A WOMAN'S WORK IS NEVER DONE

DEDICATION

When Elizabeth Andrews died, in 1960, I was a young teenager in Merthyr Tydfil, not giving a lot of thought to who I should thank for my free grammar school education, in a castle in a park, or the free university education I was being encouraged to think about, or the assiduous attention of the health service and the schools health service I had received all my life. I now know how much we all, especially in old industrial areas like south Wales, owe to the pioneers of the Labour movement like Elizabeth Andrews and her comrades, most of them now quite unknown to us.

With those debts in mind, I would like to dedicate this book to my maternal grandmother, Nellie Mourne Fitzgerald of Merthyr Vale, another early worker for socialism, unknown to history until now; also, sadly, unknown to her grandchildren, as she died of tuberculosis, that scourge of inter-war Wales which Elizabeth Andrews excoriated in her writings reprinted here.

I would also like to dedicate it to Nellie's surviving daughter, my aunt Eileen Bruynseels, with love.

Ursula Masson

Ursula Masson is a lecturer in History at the University of Glamorgan, teaching British and Welsh History in the modern period, and specialising in women's history. Her research interests are in women's political history, with publications on women in the Liberal and Labour parties, and in the suffrage movement from the late nineteenth century onwards. Ursula Masson is a founder, and current chair of Archif Menywod Cymru/Women's Archive of Wales; chair of the West of England and South Wales Women's History Network; and co-editor of *Llafur: Journal of the Welsh People's History Society.*

A WOMAN'S WORK IS NEVER DONE

AND POLITICAL ARTICLES

By Elizabeth Andrews

Edited by URSULA MASSON
With a foreword by GLENYS KINNOCK

HONNO CLASSICS

Published by Honno
'Ailsa Craig', Heol y Cawl, Dinas Powys
South Glamorgan, Wales CF6 4AH

A Woman's Work is Never Done was first published by
The Cymric Democrat Publishing Society in 1957
This edition © Honno Ltd 2006
© Introduction, Ursula Masson 2006

Reprinted November 2006

British Library Cataloguing in Publication Data

A catalogue record for this book is available from
the British Library

ISBN 1 870206 789

Published with the financial support of the Welsh Books Council

Cover image: Getty Images,

Cover design: Gwasg Gomer
Printed in Wales by Gwasg Gomer

CONTENTS

ACKNOWLEDGEMENTS

The enthusiasm of a lot of people has helped to ensure the publication of this volume. A talk on Elizabeth Andrews by Glenys Kinnock MEP on Radio Wales, and at an International Women's Day event in Cardiff, aroused a lively interest in this pioneer of women's political activity in Wales. Baroness Kinnock has added to the interest of the volume by generously supplying a Foreword. A group of trade union and labour movement women, friends and colleagues of Liz Lewis, Equalities Officer of the T&GWU, had also been organising for some time to try to get the autobiography reprinted, and they have been very supportive of this project. They supplied a scanned version of the text of *A Woman's Work is Never Done*, which unfortunately I was unable to use.

Thanks to Siân Williams and staff of the South Wales Miners' Library; Elisabeth Bennett, archivist, and staff of the South Wales Coalfield Collection; and to Vernon Jones in the Readers' Services department. at the National Library of Wales for help in locating sources.

Thanks to Lindsay Ashford, Honno Publishing Manager, and all at Honno Press.

Above all, thanks to Jane Aaron, the Honno Classics series editor, for her encouragement, support and good humoured patience; and Lowri Newman for collaboration on an earlier piece on this subject, and generous sharing of her sources this time.

ABBREVIATIONS

CWM	*Colliery Workers' Magazine*
EGAC	East Glamorgan [Labour Women's] Advisory Council
FCLWS	Free Church League for Women's Suffrage
ILP	Independent Labour Party
LW	*The Labour Woman*
NEC	[Labour Party] National Executive Committee
NUWSS	National Union of Women's Suffrage Societies
RBLP	Rhondda Borough Labour Party
RC	*Rhondda Clarion*
WCG	Women's Cooperative Guild
WFL	Women's Freedom League
WLL	Women's Labour League

Elizabeth Andrews (centre) with Violet Attlee (right), wife of
Labour Prime Minister, Clement Attlee.
Photo courtesy of the office of Glenys Kinnock MEP.

Foreword

GLENYS KINNOCK

In 1919 a 37-year-old woman from the Rhondda stood in the rarefied splendour of the King's Robing Room in the House of Lords and made a speech that would help transform the lives of women in South Wales. Giving evidence to the Sankey Commission on the mining industry, she described the hardship of colliers' wives and how pit-head baths would help them escape the drudgery that could be life threatening.

She was Elizabeth Andrews — or to the generations of women who looked to her to give them a voice, simply 'Our Elizabeth'.

Elizabeth Andrews was, in my view, a truly great Welsh woman who has sadly fallen out of our history. Elizabeth was one of the most influential female political activists and a pioneer of the early 20th century — whose contribution as a socialist, an internationalist and a suffragist has never been given the plaudits or the acknowledgement which men, who made similar contributions to Welsh life, have received. Whenever I talk about her, people are shocked that so little is known about Elizabeth. She is a forgotten heroine whose memory I believe deserves to be honoured. Publishing her book will make an enormous contribution to our efforts to put her firmly back where she belongs.

She was born in Victorian times and was still Labour Party Organiser for Wales in 1948. She campaigned for votes for women, for maternity rights and opened the first nursery school in Wales. She brought the needs of working-class women into the political arena because she shared their lives, spoke their language and voiced their hopes and fears. Yet she is the woman who the party seems to have forgotten. There is no evidence anywhere of value being placed on this memorable Welsh woman who meant so much to the women she fought for all her life.

I therefore resolved to promote greater awareness of Elizabeth's life; her story needs to be told not just because she achieved so much, but also because her life tells us the story of women of the south Wales valleys during the first half of the twentieth century.

I have campaigned for many years to re-publish Elizabeth Andrews' biography 'A Woman's Work is Never Done.' The copy I originally read was on loan from the National Library of Wales. This was before I was generously given my very own copy which I will always cherish. The book however, deserves to be read more widely.

Elizabeth Andrews' earliest political memory was of miners' leader William Abraham — known as Mabon — being elected as the first Lib-Lab MP for the Rhondda in 1885. Moving to the Rhondda at the age of 26 proved to be the catalyst for Elizabeth's true political awakening. Her interest grew from simply reading about the issues of the day, then moving on to take an active part in the political life of her community.

Elizabeth certainly didn't mind breaking tradition and she attended meetings, where she was usually the only woman. She was always given the loyal support of her husband, Thomas Andrews. Elizabeth and Thomas formed a dynamic political partnership. She had found that love, passion and politics were to go hand in hand – something I can certainly empathise with. Elizabeth and Thomas shared the same vision of a better future — where women had an equal role and where, particularly, women of the valleys were valued. But they also knew how women were suffering and how the hard, relentless work of the miners' wives and mothers was not understood, as they coped with overcrowded houses, poor sanitation and the tragically high death rates among their children.

Elizabeth went on to set up Co-operative Women's Guilds and joined the suffragist movement. She recalled the Rhondda was, in those days, 'not very safe for socialists or suffragettes'. Suffragettes were certainly never going to win a popularity contest. It's difficult to appreciate today just how hard-won their victory was. By demanding the vote they were questioning the nature of female identity and the role of women in society. Elizabeth Andrews argued that far from being a politics-free zone, the family home was where politics should begin. Her support for women's rights sat side by side with her work for her class and her community.

Elizabeth bravely stood by her conviction that women deserved to have the vote — this was not an easy position to take. She never relented and she never ceased to believe that in the family politics had to be discussed, and that all children should be protected and nurtured. She believed that only women would make the world 'fit for the child'. But, for that to happen, they had to claim their birth right — the vote.

Her socialism ran through everything she said and did and was always linked to the reality of women's lives. It had a homespun character as she linked the language which was familiar to the women she engaged with, to the need to encourage them to aspire and to fight for better conditions. For instance, she organised a demonstration in Swansea to protest about the proposal from Sir Alfred Mond, MP for Swansea and Minister for Health, to cut back on milk being provided for babies. They chanted, 'Labour women say Mond must go. Stint the milk and starve the child'. It was worth it because at the next election Mond lost his seat!

Elizabeth was the first woman to be elected, in 1916, to the Executive of the Rhondda Labour Party. And she writes movingly about the Miners' Lock Out following the General Strike. I was particularly struck by her description of 800 children from Wales who were selected from the families with the greatest needs, who were 'adopted' by families in London. She wrote, 'Our Security Committee saw to it that each child was clothed decently, so as not to be an object of pity on arrival'. How sensitive and loving and caring she was.

She openly discussed taboo subjects — pregnancy and childbirth. Her view was that 'the miner's wife runs greater risk than her man in the pit'. How little this is understood even today.

The Rhondda Council led the way, in no small part because of Elizabeth's pressure, and was prepared to initiate any maternity or child care proposals promoted by the government. But she also campaigned more widely in local authorities up and down Wales and she successfully irritated many of them! When one medical officer referred to the women's 'wild, hysterical effusions', true to form, Elizabeth was unrepentant.

Elizabeth joined forces with Rose Davies of Aberdare and this formidable duo campaigned successfully for clinics, trained midwives, home helps and telephone kiosks to give women access to medical help. The result, which was clearly acknowledged, was that precious lives were saved.

In 1935, she had another 'first' — the first nursery school in Wales was opened at Llwynpia. This is another tribute to her energy and foresight. In all things she was a woman of her times, and a woman ahead of her times.

When Elizabeth Andrews wrote her autobiography — 'A Woman's Work is Never Done' — she could not have chosen a more appropriate title. Even in retirement the woman whose personal motto was 'Educate, agitate, organise' could not abandon public duty. She became one of Wales's first women magistrates and it was predicted she could become Wales's first woman MP. That achievement may have eluded her but she held the post of Labour Party Woman Organiser for Wales for a remarkable 29 years.

It is symptomatic of all the history which has been written, which so often is **his** story, and rarely hers. I believe that her omission from our story in Wales is something which must be redressed. She achieved so much and, undaunted, she successfully challenged a culture where women did not even expect to be their own advocates.

She was skilled and different and knew it was hard 'to try and teach women not to be afraid of freedom'. She, thankfully, never was.

Despite her numerous achievements, she has never been recognised as a pioneer, a feisty woman who fought for women's rights and who cared desperately for the suffering of women in South Wales. 'Our Elizabeth' must be put firmly back into our history. I believe that the publication of her autobiography will inspire others and hopefully help to redress the balance.

Elizabeth died in 1960 at the age of 77. Following her death, the *Rhondda Leader* described her achievements and recalled the title of this autobiography: 'We can say her work is done and she did it well'. Without doubt Elizabeth's legacy lives on.

Introduction

URSULA MASSON

This volume introduces the twenty-first century reader to the writings of Elizabeth Andrews (1882-1960) 'a miner's daughter', who became a central figure in the building of the Labour Party in Wales after the First World War. Recent work on the history of the party in Wales has established Andrews' importance.[1] That friends had urged her to write the memoir is a mark of her rarity, as a woman who occupied a leading position in Welsh political life in the first half of the twentieth century. Perhaps even more importantly, she has also left a body of political journalism, much of it written in the heat of events, in the party journal, *The Labour Woman,* and in the South Wales Miners' federation monthly paper, the *Colliery Workers' Magazine* (CWM). This introduction will attempt to set these writings in their historical context.

I: Autobiography and History
A Woman's Work is Never Done can be understood in terms of a classic distinction between autobiography and memoir. According to that distinction, autobiography is essentially about the inner, the shaping of the self in time and place, its focus being 'lived and felt experience'. In the memoir, on the other hand, 'a series of events, or other factors, [dictates] the narrative course'[2]. The autobiography of Elizabeth Andrews is contained in the two short first chapters; into these are crammed the formative experiences which provided a kind of emotional and ideological capital on which she drew for the rest of her life. For social historians of the coalfield communities, Andrews has provided an invaluable picture of family life as a

source of values: values of religious faith, of 'character', and of hard work, in a harsh environment. Thereafter, the book is essentially a memoir, in which she describes her 'lifetime of service to the Labour movement', through chapters based on issues and campaigns which provide the narrative drive.

'Labour Woman'

According to the socialist historian Pamela Graves, the pioneers of Labour women's organisation shared significant characteristics:

> They had left school at fourteen or earlier and worked mostly as domestic servants or in the sewing trades. The majority were housewives and mothers. A significant percentage had been involved in the women's movement through a variety of pre-war organizations – the [Women's Labour] League, the Women's Cooperative Guild, the National Federation of Women Workers, or the Railway Women's Guild. [They] had shaped their political sensibilities around the needs and interests of women of their class.[3]

This describes some important strands in the formation of Andrews' political identity, but there were also some crucial differences: she had no children, and it is doubtful whether with such a full working life she could be meaningfully described as a housewife. Most importantly, the first two chapters of Andrews' memoir describe the construction of a very specific form of identification with class and class politics, rooted in experience and knowledge of life in the south Wales mining communities; it was this absolute identification which enabled James Griffiths to write in his foreword to the original edition that 'she does more than relate the story of her own life... [s]he has written a chapter in the history of the people of the Valleys'.[4] Andrews linked her political education, as well as the development of character and religious faith, to the home and the conditions of work and life for miners and their families. She remembered the 1885 victory celebrations for Mabon (William Abraham) on his first election to represent Rhondda, though she would have been just three years old at the time. In 1918, a newly enfranchised voter at the age of thirty-six, she was to be one of Mabon's sponsors in his final election contest. Perhaps more importantly, she recalled her political education at her father's knee. As a girl, she read the newspaper to her father, a Radical who was literate in Welsh, but not in English. She recalled reading the coverage of Hardie's victorious 1900 election campaign in Merthyr and Aberdare, when she was eighteen, as well as getting a schooling in landmarks of Labour history.

Graves leaves out of her list of the shaping experiences of Labour women the place of religious faith. The extent to which this was part of family and community life for the young Elizabeth is clear: like so many of the socialists made in Wales in the early part of the century,[5] Andrews was a product, not only of the harsh material reality of coalfield life, but also of Nonconformity, 'a key element' in the political culture.[6] If her father passed on his interest in politics, her mother's legacy was lifelong work in connection with the chapel. The relationship between Nonconformity and the developing labour movement in south Wales before the First World War was characterised by hostility from ministers and leading chapel members towards what they chose to regard as atheistical socialism. The relationship improved in the inter-war period as religion was losing its grip on the coalfield communities, but it remained one of the main streams of Andrews' life, linked always to the lessons of her childhood home, and to her marriage. Like many labour movement figures, she would argue that socialism was Christianity in practice. The languages were interchangeable: as socialists, she wrote, they 'launched out on this work with a deep conviction and missionary zeal, preaching this new gospel of Socialism and prepared to meet all opposition and difficulties'.[7] While not wishing to overstate the hold of the chapels on coalfield society after the Edwardian period, the 'intermeshing' of the Labour Party with Nonconformist culture between the wars has been noted as one of the sources of anti-Communism in the party, hostilities in which Andrews was to play her part.[8]

Andrews herself was fond of writing about the 'Three Paths' to the emancipation of the working class: 'the Trade Union Path, the Cooperative Movement Path, and the Labour Movement Path'.[9] The 'trade union path' was not an option for the majority of women in south Wales at that time, and Andrews noted that few women were present at the ILP meetings she attended, but she offered no explanation in terms of the way labour movement politics operated in the coalfield valleys before the First World War, effectively excluding women.[10] Andrews was one of the few women before 1918 who, while closely identifying herself with the available forms of women's activism, was also able to break through into the male-dominated structures. In 1916 she was to be the first woman elected to the executive of the still rather inchoate Rhondda Labour Party (later the Rhondda Borough Labour Party, RBLP).

The 'Cooperative Path' was important to Andrews: she was Secretary of Wales's first branch of the WCG, at Ton Pentre in 1914, and was responsible for the formation of a number of local branches which became the foundation for the important role the WCG played as a political and educational organisation for married women between the wars, alongside the Labour Party women's sections. As a leading member of the Guild, Andrews threw herself into the campaigns to improve maternal and child welfare provision. Like so many women of her class and generation, her upbringing and family life had given her an intimate acquaintance with the impact on women and their families of multiple births combined with poverty. The work continued throughout the inter-war period, through both the Guild and the women's sections, with energetic campaigns to persuade local authorities to fully use their powers under the 1918 Child and Maternal Welfare Act. Writing in the 1950s, Andrews took satisfaction in the reductions in maternal and infant mortality, and improved provisions of the National Health Service.

In Andrews' construction of a political identity before the First World War, the Labour and Cooperative 'paths' were joined by the feminist, in the shape of the non-militant suffrage movement. Her chapter on 'Votes for Women' is a very brief survey of the issue, from Mary Wollstonecraft in 1792 to the creation of equal voting rights for women and men in 1928, with few personal or local insights, but she joined the movement at about the same time that she got involved in the ILP and WCG: this would have put her in the company of the many hundreds of women in south Wales, of all parties and none, who belonged to the major suffrage organisation, the National Union of Women's Suffrage Societies (NUWSS), and other constitutional organisations, in addition to smaller numbers in the militant societies. She does not specify which society she joined. There was a branch of the NUWSS in Treorchy in 1911/2, and a Rhondda Fach society formed about 1912. In the neighbouring Aberdare valley, ILP women were active in the Women's Freedom League (WFL), the smaller of the militant societies which included a number of socialist women amongst its membership and leadership.[11] As closer relations were forged between the NUWSS and the Labour Party nationally a number of Rhondda ILP branches passed resolutions in support of women's suffrage in 1910-1912, and *Common Cause,* the NUWSS newspaper, sold well in the valley.[12] Andrews and her husband provided hospitality for visiting suffrage propagandists, and she remembered the Rhondda as being 'not very safe for Socialists or Suffragettes', describing the routing of 'two prominent Suffragettes'.[13]

Cardiff, Pontypridd, Aberdare and other urban centres saw similar demonstrations, as anti-suffragists and Liberal loyalists attempted to deny women the rights of the public platform and public space, in a period of deteriorating relations between the suffrage movement and the Liberal government.

It seems likely that Andrews' suffragism was linked to her ILP activity, but may also have overlapped with chapel membership, through the Free Church League for Women's Suffrage (FCLWS), formed in 1910. In February and March of 1912, Marion Phillips, then secretary of the Women's Labour League (WLL), and Annot E. Robinson, a part-time organizer for the WLL and the Fabian Women's Group, toured the Rhondda speaking on women's suffrage, as guests of the ILP and the FCLWS. Andrews was one of a number of women whom Robinson mentioned as having 'spoken and taken collections, and sold literature and done splendid work'. The women who attended the meetings were from the Liberal and Labour parties and the Free Churches (Nonconformist denominations); ILP branch secretaries (mostly, if not all male, at this time) had helped organise the events. The socialists got some mileage out of the absence of support from male Liberalism in the Rhondda, and the meetings called on Mabon, as the MP, to vote against the government's proposed new Reform Bill if women were not included.[14] The bill failed, and in any case suffragists felt they could not count on the commitment of coal-field MPs: in NUWSS records Mabon was noted as 'not quite reliable'.[15]

After the partial enfranchisement of women in 1918, the campaign for the equal franchise continued in the 1920s, though in very changed circumstances. Through her columns in the 1920s Andrews exhorted, 'Women! know your political power, treasure it, use it wisely'.[16] She urged women's sections to demand equal franchise, and writing in 1927, she welcomed the coming legislation:

It will **raise our status as Voters**, and remove that
insult to our womanhood that we got Votes because we
were **married to men**, not because we were intelligent
human beings and citizens.[17]

Andrews accepted the primary identification of women with
their maternal role and instincts; it was to be the dominant
motif in her writings during the 1920s. Indeed she developed
a view of socialist politics, local, national and international,
for both women and men, as being a politics which put the
needs and development of 'The Child' at the centre; it was
no accident that one of the women she most admired in the
Labour movement was Margaret McMillan, the influential
theorist of childhood and socialism.[18] This merging of the
private and domestic with the political is reflected in the title
of her memoir. 'A woman's work is never done' is a traditional
maxim referring to the endlessness of women's work within the
family, but Andrews' own working life, the work described in
the memoir, was outside the domestic setting. In her writings,
Andrews supported women's right to work, including the
right of married women and mothers to seek work outside the
home: she wrote, perhaps rather optimistically for the 1950s,
that the 'old idea that home and child-bearing was woman's
chief function in life has gone'.[19] At the time of her writing,
shortly after the Second World, the marriage bars on women
in teaching and the civil service were being dismantled, and
other changes initiated in wartime conditions were opening
other kinds of work to married women. However, there is
no sign that Andrews had supported the women teachers of
the Rhondda who in the 1920s challenged the marriage bar
imposed by their employer, the Labour dominated Rhondda
Urban District Council; the issue did not surface in her
monthly columns, and she may have shared the ambivalence
felt by many Labour women on this issue, faced with massive
male unemployment. But more specifically, her title affirms

her work, in the political sphere, as 'woman's work': the attempt to change the world was as essential, and as much part of women's role, as child-rearing:

> We were told when agitating for the Vote – often very patronisingly by men - that woman's place was to fit the child for the world. We retorted that … it was also her place to fit the world for the child, and before we could do either, we must take an interest in politics.[20]

Alternative Histories

Working class and Labour movement writers have used the biographical and autobiographical forms to create alternative histories, from which, however, women have largely been absent. Kenneth O. Morgan has written about 'the cult of personality' in the party, the propensity to evoke the past through praise of 'great men' and leaders.[21] Andrews created an alternative to the alternative: a labour history in which the central place was taken by women, and the struggle was for the welfare of the women and children of the working class. Minute books of Labour women's meetings in south Wales show that in addition to her role as organiser, teacher, campaigner and propagandist, she became a 'remembrancer' of women's place in Labour politics. Through her frequent reminders of the history of the party, invoking 'the early days' of women's organisation, by keeping party anniversaries, and especially by her generous naming and praising of other women who had worked for the cause, she constructed a heritage for Labour women in south Wales. This was continued in her autobiography, which is punctuated with narratives of the achievements of other women – Mrs David (Elizabeth) Williams in Swansea, Rose Davies in Aberdare, Beatrice Green and others during the 1926 lock-out. The figures commemorated by Andrews have mostly been long forgotten; they made their contribution mainly, though not exclusively, in the local setting, and would from other perspectives be invisibly embedded amongst the 'grass roots' of the party. She reminds us about the contribution of local leadership, not just in building a party, but in trying to bring about social changes which would make a real difference to the lives of working-class families.

Andrews' preface to *A Woman's Work* makes it clear that she sees it, to a great degree, as the history of the progress of women since the end of the First World war, and their progress specifically through the Labour movement. It is therefore useful to examine her account of a number of issues which have been seen by historians as indicative of the party's commitment to women and feminism. Those issues include women's suffrage in the pre-war period; and in the inter-war period, birth control and 'the endowment of motherhood', otherwise known as family allowances.

Andrews' own commitment to the political equality of men and women was not in doubt, but her gloss on the Labour movement record on women's suffrage – 'All our Labour pioneers were great fighters for the political freedom of women'– was a loyal but overly-sanguine simplification of the complex history of the relationship between the left and the movement for women's rights and citizenship. The extent to which theoretical support for women's equality was unmatched by active support in the organisations which made up the Labour movement has been explored in recent years by a number of historians.[22] Relations between the party and the NUWSS improved between 1912 and 1914, thanks to an electoral pact instigated by the Liberal-dominated NUWSS, but in the period between the wars, Labour women were strongly discouraged from membership of feminist organisations; it was a Conservative government which introduced the equal franchise, and by the end of the 1920s 'Socialism and feminism were effectively divorced'.[23]

A similar gloss characterises Andrews' recall of another campaign on behalf of women, for 'endowment of

motherhood', conducted by women's organisations including
the WCG and the WLL, together with feminist organisations,
from just before the First World War until the creation of the
Welfare State. The campaign called for a payment to women
which recognised the value of their work in the home, and
as mothers. This, it was claimed, would alleviate women's
poverty within families, and give them some measure of
independence; it would hasten the delivery of equal pay for
men and women, since payments to mothers would obviate
the necessity for, and undermine the argument for, the male
family wage. The payment finally arrived in the form of family
allowances after the Second World War. Andrews' very brief
paragraph on the subject comes near the end of Chapter X,
'The Fight For Pensions':

> It took Labour women some time to get the Party to
> accept this as policy. Trade Unionists feared that it
> would affect wages and wage negotiations. But it was
> accepted in the end and the country today enjoys the
> results of these strenuous efforts of our pioneers.

The issue had been hotly debated in the Labour movement.
Divisions were not necessarily between men and women, but
depended on views of gender responsibility in the family, and
male primacy in the world of paid work. In the 1920s, the
trade union wing of the party opposed the allowances on the
grounds that they would undermine bargaining on the basis
of a notional 'family wage', and depress male wage levels;
and the party backed away from the issue, despite support
among women members and in the ILP. As a party employee,
answerable to Marion Phillips, the Chief Woman Officer,
and ultimately to the National Executive Committee (NEC)
of the party, Andrews would herself have been unable to
support the women's position. Her only discussion of it in
her columns came in the context of the 1926 Report of the

Royal Commission on the Coal Industry, which proposed a system of 'family allowances' as part of new wage structures, thereby confirming trade unionists' fears. Setting the issue in the context of other attempts to divide the working class, Andrews warned:

> We need to be very guarded on this point. .... To adopt a family allowance under a Capitalist system with the present basis, which is nothing but a 'Fodder Basis' will violate a great Socialist principle for private gains.[24]

The other issue which tested the party's commitment to women and women's issues in the period was birth control. From 1923 to 1928, Labour women argued that birth control information should be supplied without charge at municipal Mother and Baby clinics. It was argued that this knowledge, already available to middle-class women who could pay for it, would solve the problems of poverty and chronic ill-health of working-class mothers. In recent years, historians analysing the powerlessness of women in the national party in the inter-war years, have seen birth control as the central issue around which gender tensions in the party gathered. The role of Marion Philipps, as Chief Woman Officer, was to ensure that 'the will of the vast majority of the women members' never broke through the male leadership line.[25] In Chapter VIII of *A Woman's Work*, on 'Mothers and Babies', Andrews highlighted the hideous statistics of maternal mortality from the coalfield, but made no mention of the campaigns by women in the party for dissemination of birth-control information through local clinics. Andrews never addressed the topic in her monthly columns; her report on the 1924 Labour women's conference, an uplifting account of united women 'earnest in their politics, devoted to the cause', failed to list birth control among the topics discussed, hiding it under the uncontroversial heading of 'Maternity and Child Welfare', and gave no inkling of the sometimes impassioned speeches made by delegates.[26] Her May 1925 column saw the solutions in terms of improved maternal education, welfare resources and standards of living.[27] In 1926, the NEC placed a moratorium on discussion of the issue. In February 1927 Andrews gave space in the Women's Page to an article placed by the Workers' Birth Control Group which appealed to the miners to support the women, in return for the solidarity shown in 1926.[28] They did so, overturning the ban on discussion, but the cause got no further. There were Labour women and men in south Wales who thought that birth control was a party question, and a matter of practical socialism. However, the fate of the first hospital birth-control clinic, in Abertillery, opened by Labour campaigners and closed by the opposition of the Free Church Council, exemplified the difficulties, and would have aroused Labour fears about electability.[29]

The issue highlighted the problems of the party structures set up in 1918, which, while creating women's sections and the women's organisers, also meant that the women had no power to compel the party to take notice of them.[30] Much of Andrews' work and writing during this time was dedicated to creating and invoking class solidarity, in the face of the 1926 general strike and miners' lockout and their devastating aftermath, as the articles reprinted here show. The issue of birth control threatened to split the party.

It has been suggested that that '[a]uto/biography can offer important, and much neglected insights into … the complex, and often highly ambiguous relationship between politicians and the people they claim to represent.'[31] Andrews clearly saw herself as representing the working-class women of Wales, and her rather inadequate account of the issues of women's suffrage, birth control and family allowances draws attention to the fact that to a great degree this narrative of 'a lifetime of service to the Labour movement' obscures Andrews' position in relation to the party leadership on one hand, and members on the other. As the Labour Party's first women's organiser for Wales from 1919-1948, Andrews worked under Marion Phillips, the Chief Woman Officer of the party from 1918-1931, and then under Mary Sutherland. Andrews described many aspects of her work as an organiser, and this is one of the features of the memoir which makes it so valuable as political history. Writing from the perspective of the 1950s, she made light of what must often have been difficult, tiring and lonely work. The organisation of labour women in Wales before the First World War had been weak; by 1918 south Wales had only three branches of the WLL, in Cardiff, Swansea and Newport. By the end of the 1920s, East Glamorgan, including Rhondda, had ninety-five sections. By 1933, more than 9,000 women formed 45 per cent of the individual party membership in Wales, and by the time of Andrews' retirement in 1948 the number had increased to 12,814, though the proportion of women had fallen.[32] While Andrews clearly felt less at home in the country beyond the coalfield, by the time she retired, north Wales had two advisory councils supporting and coordinating the work of sections. Such a level of organisation was a remarkable achievement, considering the weakness of pre-war organisation throughout Wales; the tireless work undertaken by Andrews to the end of her career is reflected in the regular reports from Wales to *The Labour Woman.*

However, the position of women's organiser *was* an ambiguous one, and Andrews forbore from comment on her working relationship with her superiors, or direct comment on her role in relation to them and the NEC. In *A Woman's Work,* Andrews represented her role as directed towards the interests of women and communities in Wales. But both she and Phillips were party appointees, and the 1918 constitution made it clear that the women's officers' 'first loyalty was to the party leadership, which was overwhelmingly male'[33] As Graves has shown, Phillips 'consistently supported the party line, and worked hard to discourage "dissident" women'.[34]

Presumably, this 'discouragement' might need to be passed down the line through the regional women's officers too. The paucity of references to the national structures of the Party which was her employer helped to maintain the focus of the memoir as 'the history of the people of the Valleys', and it was a story of steady progress and improvement for the working class in the care of the Labour Party. each chapter of the memoir expressing this movement, ending on an upward note. 'That is the Socialist Way to Progress' are the final words of her chapter on 'Women in the Labour Party', which ends with the election victory of 1945 and the creation of the welfare state. The organisation of *A Woman's Work* in short chapters dealing with a series of campaigns directed to the good of the communities she identified with - the pit-head baths campaigns, the attempt to beat TB through pressure on local authorities, the implementation of the 1918 Child and Maternal Welfare Act, nursery schools, pensions – also allowed her to avoid dealing with dissension in the party: the Party crises of the 1930s, for example, feature nowhere in her account.

It might fairly be argued that writing in the context of post-war achievement by Labour, and at the end of an impressive career, Andrews may well have felt that the old disagreements and controversies could be forgotten. The 1945 landslide wiped out the bitterness of the 1930s; the creation of a national health service and the introduction of family allowances seemed to promise to do for women what the party had shied away from in the 1920s, and weakened the appeal of Communism. But for present-day readers, as students of history, and especially of the progress of women in the Labour party, it is important to set Andrews' writings in the context of recent historical analyses, which inevitably take a more critical line than she did herself.

II Political Journalism 1923-1948
Most of Andrews' political journalism was produced in the

1920s and the 1930s. As women's organiser for the party in Wales, she submitted a monthly report to the section 'Women's Work in the Districts' in the party journal *The Labour Woman,* from 1920 to her retirement in 1947. For the most part, these were lists of activities and events of the advisory councils and sections; occasionally they indicated the conditions in which women's party activities were being carried on, for example, as the impact on members of bombing raids during the Second World War. Perhaps half-a-dozen times over the years, Andrews contributed a longer feature, on organizational matters or on specifically Welsh issues. For historians of the Labour Party in Wales as a whole, these are invaluable sources. Her other major outlet for political propagandising, exhortation and information was the monthly SWMF publication *Colliery Workers' Magazine,* published 1923-1927, for which she edited the regular 'Women's Page'. She wrote most of the material herself, but in a significant number of cases, other women active in the coalfield also contributed. Andrews would have had in mind different target readerships for the two publications. *Labour Woman* circulated to party members and her occasional articles on Welsh matters had the air of informing the outside world on special conditions. The 'Women's Page' in *CWM* was aimed, not necessarily at party members, but as her first article (reprinted here) shows, at 'wives and mothers' of colliery workers.

Andrews' by-line appeared in various forms on these articles: usually, her authority as 'Organiser' or 'National Organiser' was invoked. Her status as JP was always included – she had become one of Wales's first women JPs in 1920, and was to serve on the bench of magistrates in Ystrad until a year before her death. This gave her the platform to write on juvenile delinquency, and to call for the abolition of capital punishment, an article written in the thick of international furore over the convictions for murder and death sentences on the Italian anarchists Sacco and Vanzetti, in the United States.[35]

For the most part, however, the articles in the *CWM* addressed coalfield issues, including those she produced throughout the strike and lockout of 1926. In support of her ideas, she would quote from the latest research and statistics, but was just as likely to quote from the bible, and from literature; Tolstoy, Williams Morris, Ella Wheeler Wilcox, Robert Browning, Robert Lowell were all mined for apposite and moving lines.

It has not been possible to reprint all of Andrews' writings from these years. In making a selection, the criteria have been that they should indicate the breadth of Andrews writing, the passion of which she was capable, and her partisanship; and that they should address social and political issues of her day particularly affecting women, rather than party organisational matters which are now of less interest except to students of party history. Her first columns in the *CWM* began with the crisis of poverty and its impact on mining families, with women bearing the brunt. She wrote on the need to revive the campaign for pit-head baths, on which progress was painfully slow. She linked the need for improved conditions at the pit to improved health and standard of life for families, and especially for women: as in her testimony to the Sankey Commission in 1919,[36] she made the link between the poor health of women, and especially the high rate of miscarriages, and their work for miners – or, as she put it in 1923, for the mineowners. In 1924, during the cautious optimism of Labour's first short-lived term in office, she responded to a Housing Bill with a description of needs in Wales which drew on her knowledge of the rural as well as the industrial areas. In 1925, writing on the importance of local government, she called for the supply of clean milk to combat TB, and for improved maternity services and open-air nurseries. In 1939, at the end of a decade when unemployment and poverty had bitten deeper into working-class communities and the incidence of the disease in Wales had risen, while it declined in Britain generally,[37] she was still writing about 'Wales and Her Poverty', still calling for clean milk, a pure water supply, decent housing and a wide array of social services, as she responded to a Ministry of Health report on tuberculosis in Wales. It did not require a Beveridge Report for women in working-class communities to know what was needed for 'the Right to Live'.

Like many on the left and left-of-centre in the 1920s and 1930s, Andrews supported anti-war efforts. She believed that women had a specific contribution to make; their motherly 'instinct of preservation', their need to 'fit the world to the child', would be a valuable weapon introduced into mainstream politics. These ideas were pervasive in the women's movements for peace of the 'twenties in which the WCG was prominent, and in the work of the League of Nations Union, which Andrews supported. The 1924 article reprinted here was prompted by developments in the League in devising protocols for international arbitration in which Ramsay MacDonald had been instrumental. In 1927 Andrews herself attended a League of Nations conference at the International Labour Office in Geneva. By 1938, writing on 'Bread and Peace' in *The Labour Woman*, as European nations re-armed, she wrote about the poverty of families in Japan and Germany as well as Britain, calling for the beating of swords into ploughshares, still hopeful for some role for the League.

As far as party politics were concerned, Andrews was no pacifist, despite the judgement of an obituarist that one of her chief characteristics was 'equanimity'.[38] She relished the fight against class enemies, and delighted in the electoral victories which came fairly regularly in south Wales in the 1920s. Organising women's sections for electoral work was an important part of her job, and she savoured the defeat of Liberals in north and south Wales. She used her *CWM* column to rouse women to greater electoral efforts, and this was to yield satisfying results in the general election of 1924, which saw the return of the first, albeit short-lived, Labour government led by Ramsay MacDonald. The 1920s were dominated by the impact of the depression and of industrial troubles. As wages fell and unemployment rose in the coal industry, the bitter and lengthy disputes of 1921 and 1926 defined the decade. In 1926 women from the mining districts came into their own as they organised in support of the strike, and their efforts – at least in the more law-abiding activities[39] - were led by Andrews with her usual energy. Between April 12 and May 13, she addressed twenty meetings of over 10,000 women, rallying support for the miners and recruiting women into the party at the same time. She used her monthly column in the *CWM* to make impassioned appeals to women in the coalfield for 'unity, loyalty, and faith in our cause, and in each other'. Women in the coalfield were being targeted by Flora Drummond's anti-socialist Women's Guild of Empire; Andrews urged mass meetings of miners' wives 'to counter [the Guild's] mischievous activities'.[40] In a series of columns during the strike and lockout, a selection of which are reprinted here, Andrews and other women explained the issues and vividly conjured a 'spirit of Comradeship and Fellowship … kindness, love and sympathy' amongst the strikers and their communities.

Andrews was disturbed by the outcome of the strike, and its likely long-term impact on families and communities. She described the dispute as 'Industrial War', which like the 1914-18 war, had 'maimed' the combatants, and especially 'thousands of our young mothers and babies'[41]. To prevent another such war, she argued for 'a newer conception' of politics, a model for which was provided by the work of the women's committees during the lock-out, which put the needs of children at the centre of their efforts. 'If we could only approach all our Economic, Social, National and International problems from this point of view, making the **welfare of the child the basis of human relationship in Human Society,** we would soon solve these problems'.[42] Above all the it was the experience of the lock-out, of the spirit of collectivity expressed particularly through the women's actions, which prefigured, for Andrews, a 'New Era'. However, she was more than ready, in 1935, to urge women to throw themselves into another 'industrial war …a war against Poverty. A just demand, so that miners get a square deal,' and to call again for 'hundred per cent loyalty'.[43]

Writing in the short-lived RBLP paper, *Rhondda Clarion*, she used the same article, 'A Clarion Call - to the Rhondda Women', to attack the tactics of Communist councillors. From the bitter end of the 1926 lock-out, relations between Labour and the Communists in the Rhondda deteriorated.[44] Andrews recalled the period in her memoir, referring to personal attacks by the CP on her and others. The seriousness with which the party viewed the challenge from the CP, and its possible appeal to women, is suggested by the number of times Andrews returned to the subject in her writing and in the women's conferences in the 1930s and 1940s. In 1937, at a conference of the East Glamorgan Advisory Council, Andrews appealed for loyalty in the sections, 'for the women not to be led away with the United Front'.[45] During the Second World War, the Communist-led People's Vigilance Committees and the 'Women's Parliament' beckoned to political women, as Andrews held the line, appealing again to loyalty. The decline of Communism in the Rhondda in the post-war period, which she attributed to improvements in the condition and welfare of the working class, gave her nothing but satisfaction.

One of Andrews' last columns in the *CWM* was headed "Votes for Women", the quotation marks suggesting the revival of a well-worn slogan. While the campaigns for the equal franchise had continued during the 1920s, women's organisations had increasingly put the needs of working-class wives and mothers at the centre of their arguments, and Andrews characteristically dismisses journalistic representations of the 'Flapper vote' to remind her working-class readers that equality was in their interest as wives, mothers, and workers. She will have taken no pleasure in welcoming a Tory bill, so qualified her delight at the prospect of political equality with a note of distrust: 'Tory promises are like pie-crusts – made to be broken'.

Andrews' valedictory article in *The Labour Woman* was mainly about the organisational history of Welsh party women. It seems appropriate to include her own review of her political career, written at a moment of optimism, when it seemed as she wrote, that 'so many of the things we worked for, hoped for, and prayed for, are achieved or about to be achieved'. Again characteristically, she gave advice on work still to be done, and looked forward to more work herself.

In 1949, after her retirement as organiser, and the award of OBE, Andrews contested the Ton Pentre ward for the Labour Party in the County Council elections. It was expected to be a close run thing, but she was soundly beaten by the sitting councillor, an Independent. The local newspaper questioned the wisdom of putting up for 'the exacting work of the County Council' a candidate past retirement age.[46] But Andrews had ten energetic years of work in front of her, as chairman of the Ystrad magistrates, as a member of the Glamorgan Health Executive Council, the Pontypridd and Rhondda Hospital Management Committee, and of a Home Office committee to a local probation hostel. She remained active in her chapel, the Bethany Church and Mission in Gelli. In March 1959, Andrews attended her last Labour women's advisory council to pay tribute to 'our dear beloved Alderman Rose Davies', who had been her comrade in the party almost from the beginning. A year later, the council stood in silent tribute to 'our beloved Elizabeth'. She had died, aged 77, after fracturing her femur in a fall as she entered a meeting of the Health Executive Council. A colleague said at her funeral, 'we can say her work is done, and she did it well'. Andrews would have replied, 'there is still much work to be done'.[47]

Footnotes

[1] Neil Evans and Dot Jones, ' "To Help Forward the Great Work of Humanity": Women in the Labour Party in Wales', in Duncan Tanner, Chris Williams and Deian Hopkin (eds) T*he Labour Party in Wales 1900-2000* (Cardiff, 2000); Dot Jones, 'Andrews, Elizabeth (1882-1960)', *Oxford Dictionary of National Biography*, Vol. 2 (Oxford 2004) 121; Lowri Newman, 'A Distinctive Brand of Politics: Women in the South Wales Labour Party 1918-1939', unpublished MPhil dissertation, University of Glamorgan, 2003; Ursula Masson and Lowri Newman, 'Andrews, Elizabeth (1882-1960): Labour Party Women's Organiser for Wales', in Keith Gildart, David Howell and Neville Kirk (eds), *Dictionary of Labour Biography*, Volume XI (Basingstoke, 2003) 1-11. Extracts from *A Woman's Work is Never Done* have been reprinted in Carol White and Sian Rhiannon Williams (eds), *Struggle or Starve: Women's lives in the South Wales valleys between the two World Wars* (Dinas Powys 1998).

[2] Carolyn Steedman, *Childhood, Culture and Class in Britain: Margaret McMillan, 1860-1931* (New Brunswick, 1990) 246-7.

[3] Pamela Graves, 'An Experiment in Women-Centred Socialism: Labour Women in Britain', in Helmut Gruber and Pamela Graves (eds), *Women and Socialism, Socialism and Women: Europe Between the Two World Wars* (Oxford 1998), 207.

[4] James Griffiths MP, 'Foreword', to Andrews, *A Woman's Work.*

[5] For a discussion of the use of the terms 'socialist woman', and 'labour woman' see June Hannam & Karen Hunt, *Socialist Women: Britain 1880s-1920s* (London, 2002) 8-12.

[6] Richard Lewis, 'Political Culture and Ideology 1900-1918', in Tanner *et al.* (eds) *The Labour Party in Wales,* 90.

[7] Andrews, *A Woman's Work*, 13.

[8] Chris Williams, *Democratic Rhondda: Politics and Society 1885-1951* (Cardiff, 1996) 114-5, 198-9, 241, fn. 29; Andrews, *op.cit.* 1-2, 19; *Labour Woman (LW)*, March 1960; *Rhondda Clarion (RC)*, October 1935.

[9] *Colliery Workers' Magazine (CWM)* January 1925, 21; Andrews, *A Woman's Work,* 42-3.

[10] Chris Williams, *Capitalism, Community and Conflict: The South*

Wales Coalfield 1898-1947 (Cardiff 1998), 112.

[11] Ursula Masson, 'Davies, Florence Rose (1882-1958)', in Gildart *et al.*, *Dictionary* 39-40; *eadem* (ed.), *Women's Rights and Womanly Duties: the Aberdare Women's Liberal Association 1891-1910* (Cardiff 2005) 76-8.

[12] Ursula Masson, 'Divided Loyalties: Women's Suffrage and Party Politics in South Wales 1912-1915', *Llafur: Journal of Welsh Labour History,* Vol. 7, Nos. 3 & 4, 1998-9, 120.

[13] Andrews, *A Woman's Work*, Ch.II.

[14] *Rhondda Socialist* (*RS*), February-March 1912.

[15] Masson, 'Divided Loyalties', *passim*.

[16] *CWM* May 1925.

[17] *CWM* May 1927, emphasis original.

[18] Andrews, *A Woman's Work*, Ch.IX.

[19] Andrews, *A Woman's Work*, 11.

[20] *Ibid*.

[21] Kenneth O. Morgan, *Labour People: Hardie to Kinnock* (Oxford 1992) 1-2; Jon Lawrence, *Speaking for the People: Party, Language and Popular Politics in England, 1867-1914* (Cambridge, 1998) 228-9, 258.

[22] For example, Karen Hunt, *Equivocal Feminists: the Social Democratic Federation and the woman question 1884-1911* (Cambridge, 1996); Hannam & Hunt, *Socialist Women*, 22-4.

[23] Graves, 'An Experiment', 182.

[24] *CWM* April 1926 (emphasis original).

[25] Graves, 'An Experiment', 186.

[26] *CWM* June 1924.

[27] *CWM* May 1925.

[28] *CWM* February 1927.

[29] Margaret Douglas, 'Women, God and Birth Control: the first hospital birth control clinic, Abertillery, 1925', *Llafur: Journal of Welsh Labour History*, Vol. 6, No. 4, 1995, 110-122.

[30] Graves, 'An Experiment', 198.

[31] Lawrence, *Speaking for the People,* 229.

[32] Evans & Jones, 'To Help Forward the Great Work of Humanity', 220-1.

[33] Graves, 'An Experiment', 186.

[34] Ibid.

[35] *CWM*, February 1926: 'The Young Delinquent'; September 1927: 'Why Capital Punishment should be Abolished'. Andrews wrote that '[a]t the time of writing this article we do not know what may happen', but the men had been executed before her article went to print.

[36] Royal Commission on the Coal Industry Commission, Vol. 2, Reports and Minutes of Evidence 1919, 1019ff.

[37] Deirdre Beddoe, *Out of the Shadows: A History of Women in Twentieth Century Wales* (Cardiff, 2000) 22-3, 97; White and Williams (eds), *Struggle or Starve,* 19-20.

[38] *LW* March 1960.

[39] For women's involvement in picketing, protests and clashes with the authorities which saw a number of them in court, Hywel Francis and David Smith, *The Fed: a History of the South Wales Miners in the Twentieth Century* (London 1980) Ch. 2.

[40] Minutes, East Glamorgan Advisory Council (EGAC), 6 March 1926. 'General' Flora Drummond had been a leading member of the militant suffrage organisation, the Women's Social and Political Union (WSPU) before the war, but like its leaders, Emmeline and Christabel Pankhurst, had become ultra-patriotic during the war, and increasingly right wing afterwards.

[41] *CWM* December 1926, January 1927.

[42] *Ibid,* emphasis in original.

[43] *RC*, October 1925.

[44] Williams, *Democratic Rhondda*, Ch. 5.

[45] Minutes EGAC annual conference 1937.

[46] *Rhondda Leader (RL),* 9 April 1949.

[47] *RL,* 30 January 1960; *A Woman's Work*, 31

ELIZABETH ANDREWS : KEY DATES

1910-1914: Married Thomas Tyde Andrews; joined the Independent Labour Party; helped form the first Women's Co-operative Guilds in the Rhondda; joined the women's suffrage movement.

1916: The first woman to be elected to the Executive of the Rhondda Borough Labour Party.

1914-1918: Served on the War Pensions Committee and the Disablement Training Committee in the Rhondda.

1918: Worked for miners' candidates in the General Election. Was able to vote in a general election for the first time, at the age of 37.

1919: Appointed Labour Party Woman Organiser for Wales; appointed member of the Ministry of Health Welsh Consultative Council, surveying health services in Wales; gave evidence at the Sankey Committee on the mining industry in pit head baths and housing in mining areas.

1920: Appointed amongst the first women JPs.

1920-1930: Building Labour Party women's organisation throughout Wales. Editor, 'The Women's Page', *CWM*.

1927: Attended League Of Nations peace conference at International Labour Office in Geneva.

1931: Visited the International Socialist Congress in Vienna - the first since 1914-18 war.

1935: Visited Sweden with a party of Labour Women

1939-1945: Second World War : Liaison Officer for Women's side of the Labour Party in Wales on Wartime Committees of the Ministry of Information, Board of Trade, Ministry of Fuel and Power and Ministry of Food.

1946: Death of Tom Andrews.

1947: Retired as Labour Woman Organiser for Wales at the end of the year.

1948-1959: Member, Ministry of Health Executive Council; Pontypridd and Rhondda Hospital Committee; Home Office committee for 'House of Trees' Salvation Army Probation Hostel, Williamstown, Rhondda.

1949: Awarded OBE; stood unsuccessfully in local elections.

1960: January, died aged 77.

* * *

Her Favourite Quotation:

> Politics is not a game, but a concentration of the best intelligence and feeling of the nation upon the gravest issues in national life ... To uplift the race, assuage suffering, mitigate poverty, and do battle with old evils is the finest thing that can happen to a woman when she is enlisted actively and responsibly in that great crusade.
>
> Joseph McCabe, *Woman in Political Evolution*

Her personal motto: Educate, agitate, organise!

A WOMAN'S WORK
IS
NEVER DONE

DEDICATED

To the memory of my husband whose devoted
partnership and encouragement meant so much
to me in all my public life.

FOREWORD

'Mrs. Andrews — our Organiser': This is how the writer of these reminiscences was known to the successive generations of Labour women in the Valleys of Wales. And they said '*our Organiser*' with pride and affection. For Mrs. Andrews shared their life, spoke their language and voiced their hopes — and fears.

So that in turning the pages of memory she does more than relate the story of her own life — the devoted life of service and endeavour. She has written a chapter in the history of the people of the Valleys; the days of childhood in the miners' home at Hirwaun — one of eleven nurtured on the hearth warmed by our peasant culture; those early struggles of women for a place in the life of the community; the campaigns for votes for women and pit-head baths and for maternity and child welfare; and then the call to service in the work of our Party and the building of our Women's Sections. What a debt of gratitude we owe them — the 'hewers of wood' in the work of our movement!

In these pages we read of the life of the women of the Valleys in sunshine and shadow; how hope was kept alive in the dark days of the depression and of how at long last, there came the days of our triumph.

For the older readers these pages will bring badck nostalgic memories of the struggles of yesterday. To the younger readers they will serve as an inspiration for the tasks of tomorrow.

JIM GRIFFITHS

James Griffiths (1890-1975), MP for Llanelli 1936-1970, was a cabinet minister in the Labour governments 1945-51, responsible for shaping national insurance policy, now regarded as one of the architects of the post-war Welfare

State. In opposition at time of writing this foreword, he was later (1964-66) the first Secretary of State to the newly-created Welsh Office, in Harold Wilson's government. — UM

A Preface — and a Message

I have been urged by many of my colleagues to write a short story of my own life and activities and especially of my work as the first Labour Woman Organiser for Wales from 1919 – 1948.

They wished me to record the changes that have taken place in the lives of our people, especially those of women and children in this last half century. This I have done in my book.

Having been born in the reign of Queen Victoria and lived the first twenty years of my life under the rigid and narrow outlook of that era on woman's place in society, I can perceive the revolutionary change that has taken place in the life of women in every sphere of activity today. I am glad to have been given the opportunity to play a small part in helping these changes to come about.

The changes in the last thirty years have been tremendous: from 'Poverty in the midst of Plenty' to the Welfare State and Full Employment is nothing short of a great Social revolution. The general outlook on a Woman – as wife and mother, as worker and citizen, and her status in the scheme of things has altered in a way of undreamt of at the beginning of this century.

Her place in the home, industry, the professions and in public nationally and internationally has been completely changed ; her outlook on dress, furnishing, homemaking, and the education and welfare of her children has moved towards new horizons.

The advent of science in the home and industry and in

everyday life calls for further training in this new age, and in addition for men and women with ability and sense of responsibility as workers and citizens.

The younger generation of today who are enjoying these hard won privileges and personal freedom get very impatient with their parents and older people when they relate past struggles. But it is from the ruins and suffering of the past that we have built the present, and the future will depend on what we do now.

Although we have experienced two World Wars and their aftermath, and years of scarcity and restriction in the first half of this century, historic changes have taken place. While War destroys precious lives and much that is best, it also burns up a lot of rubbish — including old ideas. After each war reconstruction plans bring about the drastic changes which conditions call for. However, we all hope in the next half of this century we shall not need war to bring about great changes, and that our democracy will be so educated and people will so use their power as citizens that nations will learn that reason, understanding, and goodwill are wiser and safer than atomic bombs. So will they learn to live together in peace and concord.

It is by looking backwards that we can see the road we have travelled. Our pioneers blazed the trail and made the sacrifices that have brought us so far. Let us face the future with courage and determination. Never let us betray those pioneers by indifference and apathy and by this modern 'could not care less' attitude in our responsibility as workers and citizens.

In my work as Organiser I was often asked – 'Whatever do you women discuss at your meetings?' – and I was told by many good comrades that the women met just for teas and gossip. But if that was all we did in the early days we would never have trained and equipped so many able women who have played their part in public life and in the Labour

Movement.

The Women's Sections and Advisory Councils have served as the Working Women's University. I hope that this short record will inspire the younger generation to carry on the educational work in the Movement. For 'Knowledge is Power' and Socialism calls for the best from us all.

Chapter One
I was a Miner's Daughter

I WAS born on December 15th, 1882, at Hirwaen, Breconshire, near Aberdare, one of a family of eleven children – four boys and seven girls. I was the third child. One baby sister died when a few weeks old, and one brother died in his teenage; the other nine reached maturity and all married.

My father Samuel Smith was a miner. When his father was killed on the railway, grandmother was left with five young children. How well I remember her in her black lace cape and shawl and lilac print apron. She looked so neat and dignified. She loved her small garden and I learnt much from her about flowers as a child.

My mother Charlotte was one of five sisters left motherless, so the girls had to go out to domestic service at an early age for little more than their keep. Long hours, hard work and poor conditions were their lot. Two of her sisters married iron workers and migrated to America, where ironworks and steelworks were developing and held out great promise. Many families left South Wales for America in those early days.

My father died at the age of fifty-seven from silicosis, known in those days 'miners' asthma', and I have lost two brothers since then from the same disease.

Father was a very devout Christian, and set us all a good example; his wise guidance and advice we all treasured. I often think of the eavesdropping I did when young outside father's bedroom to listen to him praying aloud asking for guidance, and committing us to God's care and help. He taught us, too, not to waste bread, by telling us the story of the 'hungry forties'.

I was the first child to leave home and well I remember his advice – 'Treasure your character, it is the most precious thing you have: remember this – no one can break it for you unless you yourself break it first'. I often used this challenge when fighting the Communists in the early days when they thought little of attacking me personally.

Mother lived until she was eighty-six and was alert up to within three years of her passing. She took a keen interest in religious work. The Welsh family Bible with its coloured plates was a favourite book in our home and Mother would spend hours with us children on Sunday nights explaining very vividly the Biblical stories. In the centre of this bible on a few illuminated pages, the birth, marriages and deaths of the family were recorded. *The first Births Notification Act only came in in 1907 and an extension of this Act for compulsory notification was passed in 1915* so you can understand how the Bible was treasured in our homes.

Both Father and Mother learnt to read Welsh in Sunday School. We were all christened in Zoar Welsh Wesleyan Chapel, Hirwaun, and we all had to take part in the Chapel activities: Sunday School, Band of Hope, Young People's Guild and local Eisteddfodau.

I commenced school when I was about four years old and I remember taking my two pennies every Monday to pay for it. Small children under five paid 2d. or 1/- for a family. I loved school from an early age.

Looking back to those days under the old School Board when conditions were appalling – bad sanitary arrangements, poor ventilation, no provision for drying clothes, and poor water supply – one can make a comparison with today's modern Schools and modern methods of teaching, and realise the revolution that has taken place in our educational system.

I had a great desire to become a teacher. My ambition was favoured by my Headmistress and I was often sent to help in the Infant School when I was in the upper standards. I had to leave school at twelve owing to our large family and the coming ninth baby. This baby sister died and I had a chance to return to school for another year. My school career ended at thirteen when I had passed the seventh standard.

Two years after leaving school I attended the first evening classes held in the village. At the end of the session I carried away two first prizes for the best essay and for the best pie! The Inspector was very interested in my essay and asked the Headmistress to try and get my parents to agree for me to return to school to be trained as a teacher. But my parents could not afford the trainfare to travel to Aberdare for higher education. They also needed my help at home with three miners at work and six children attending school. The washing, ironing, cooking and mending were endless and the hard times, low wages and strikes made it very difficult for us all. Babies arrived every two years and being the eldest girl, I had to be a little mother. There was little chance of playing after school hours unless I had a baby in my arms. Prams were rare those days in working class homes; babies were nursed in shawls. My two elder brothers were part-time in school and part-time in the pit.

School examinations took place once a year when the Inspectors and members of the School Board attended, and it was a day of all days for us children. We were turned out in our Sunday-best frocks with white embroidered pinafores. The School was spick and span for the occasion. My school frock was black and grey striped Welsh flannel, with brown holland pinafore, bound with pink and blue binding, well starched. I wore naily boots.

Well I remember pleading with mother to let me have a cashmere frock and non-naily boots for school! Mother told me she could not afford it, because she had to see to it that we were well fed to give us healthy bodies, and that we 'could have our fineries when we were old enough to earn for ourselves'.

We always had Sunday-best frocks that were passed down to the younger ones when we had outgrown them. Luckily for us Mother was a good needlewoman and a good cook. She would sew until the early hours of the morning to keep us tidy. She bought a sewing machine to help her, and I learnt to sew at a very early age.

My father mended our boots and the family had to help with an allotment, so that we grew most of our vegetables. We also rented a perch of land from a local farmer to grow enough potatoes for the winter. These were stored in mounds of earth in the back garden. The cooking, washing, bathing and the drying of pit clothes had to be done in the kitchen; the fire had to be kept in all night in an open grate.

When very young I had to help to mend the pit clothes. This was hard work. The needle and thread had to be waxed for nearly every stitch before I could get it into the moleskin. This job often kept us at it until the early hours of the morning because of the long hours the miners worked.

Our only relaxation was on Sunday where we all turned out to Chapel and Sunday School. It was a pleasure to see the miners and their families in their Sunday best. The blue scars on their hands and faces were the only mark they carried of their trade.

I marvel at the way our parents managed to rear decent families in the latter part of the last century, and the beginning of this century, especially during periods of strikes. I remember one strike lasting six months, the only income being a small strike pay from the Miner's Federation. But the women stood loyally by their menfolk in their struggle for higher pay, shorter hours and better conditions. The Masters tried to starve them into submission.

The miners were then paid fortnightly and the first call on the pay in my home was rent, sick fund and Miners' Federation. This gave my parents some sense of security against sickness and strikes, and great sacrifices had to be made to keep up the payments. Many sickness clubs were formed in those days in the mining areas and Insurance companies thrived. There was a real dread of being buried by the Poor Law in a pauper's grave.

I remember a favourite refrain to a recitation on 'the Pauper's Grave' heard at our penny readings and concerts –

>*'Rattle his bones over the stones*
>*He is only a Pauper that no one owns'*

It had a great effect on the audience.

In 1884 my parents moved from Hirwaun to Mardy, Rhondda. My father was one of the rescued from the Mardy explosion in 1885. After this they moved back to Hirwaun. We children loved to hear the way my Mother and Father related their experiences of this explosion and the way my father and his mates escaped. To make it more vivid to us, Father would draw a plan of the pit in chalk on the kitchen floor. This made a lasting impression on our young minds. The courage, faith and comradeship that exists among miners, especially in peril, is worthy to be told.

Chapter Two
The School of Life

WILLIAM ABRAHAM (better known as 'Mabon') was the miners' leader in my young days. In 1885 he became the first Lib-Lab Member of Parliament for Rhondda.

It was the first election after the miners got the vote. A committee had been formed in the Rhondda to secure Mabon as their candidate but the 'Liberal 300' would have nothing to do with him. They brought forward Mr. Fred Davies, a twenty-two year old colliery owner as Liberal Candidate. The Liberals accused Mabon of being a 'Tory in disguise'. They did not think Mabon — 'notwithstanding his abilities and good record' — was a suitable working class candidate! But Mabon won and the news caused great excitement. Although very young, I have some recollection of the great crowd, and Mabon being carried by the miners singing '*Mabon yw y Dyn*' ('*Mabon is the Man*'). All the houses were lit up with candles in each window to celebrate the victory.

Years after, when I got my first vote in 1918, I was privileged to be a seconder of Mabon's candidature for the General Election. It was his last fight for Parliament.

After he became MP his name soon became a household word. He fought for the first Monday in the month to be a holiday for miners. It became known as 'Mabon's Day' and was greatly appreciated owing to the long hours miners had to work. During winter months they rarely saw daylight except on Sunday. They had miles to walk to work and often miles to walk underground. Accidents were numerous. There were no buses, pit baths, canteens, ambulances or hospitals. The injured were carried home on stretchers and often operations had to be performed on kitchen tables with an oil lamp for light.

There was no provision for accidents at the pit top, no decent wage and very little concern about the safety and health of the men. Explosions were common and many precious lives were lost. It was only when explosions took place that public sympathy was aroused for the miner and his family.

James Grifftiths, M.P., when he was Miners' Agent, summed up the position very aptly when he said that the public:

'Weeps for them when there is an explosion
 Curses them, when there is a strike
 And forgets them the rest of the time'.

I became very interested in politics when very young for Father was a Radical. He could only read Welsh and I used to read all the news to him. I was too young to understand what it was all about but I remember some outstanding incidents such as the Taff Vale Strike, the Tichbourne case and Osborne Judgment. I read him all the Election news when Keir Hardie fought the old East Glamorgan Division which included the Merthyr and Aberdare Divisions.

My first experience of writing a paper on a religious topic for our Wesley Guild was an ordeal. I wrote the paper but was so nervous at the thought of reading it that I made myself ill and was not able to attend. The Minister had to read it for me. I realised in this first experience how the mind can affect us physically. It taught me to be very patient and understanding when training women to take part in public work for the first time.

In 1904 I had the experience of writing my first letter to the Press. It was during the Welsh Revival. A controversy had arisen in the Press when a well-known Non-conformist Minister condemned the revival of Evan Roberts as 'mass emotionalism'. Letters began to pour in to the evening paper.

My letter favoured the revival. I only put my initials to it, so there was much guessing in our village about who wrote it.

In the early days the only outside work for girls in our village was the Brickworks or the Colliery Screens. I was terrified that I would be sent to either of them. But when I was seventeen I was sent to learn dressmaking for twelve months. We had to pay 10/- a quarter for learning the trade. At that time dressmakers went out to the homes of the people to sew and were paid 1/6 to 2/- a day and their meals, and carried their own sewing machine. When I was nineteen I launched out with my own workroom and had two apprentices. In 1905 I left home to take charge of a workroom in a shop at Llanwrtyd Wells. Mother was very unwilling to let me leave home and gave me little encouragement by saying that I would be 'back home in a few weeks'.This however only made me more determined to make a success of this venture, and I stayed there three years. My salary was £30 a year, living in, and having my clothes cost price.

In 1908 I decided I would try and get into a larger business. I applied for three posts, two in Manchester the other in Ystrad Rhondda. I had a favourable reply from the three but I chose Ystrad because it was nearer home. It was a flourishing business ; it had large workrooms and a number of apprentices. I received £40 a year, living in, and clothes at cost price. But we had to work sixty-eight hours a week, and shops were open until midnight on Saturday night in those days.

It was in the Rhondda that I became keenly interested in politics and public work for the Church and Sunday School. It was here I met my husband Thomas T. Andrews. He had worked in the mines for several years, but had given it up for Insurance. He was a great reader and keenly interested in the Independent Labour Party, being one of five that formed the first branch of the I.L.P. in the Rhondda. I attended political meetings with him before our marriage and often found that I was the only woman present.

We were married on June 15th, 1910. Our married life was a real partnership. We were interested in the same social and religious problems. I owe him so much for his devoted loyalty and for the inspiration and encouragement he gave me in my public work.

He was the first secretary of the I.L.P. and I helped him with the work. Our home had an ever-open door to all I.L.P. speakers and Suffragettes that came to the Valley. We were very privileged to entertain some of our noblest pioneers.

I joined the Co-operative Movement after marriage and became interested in developing Women's Guilds in the Rhondda. When the first Guild was formed at Tom Pentre in 1914, I was appointed first Secretary. I also joined the Suffrage Movement (non-militant).

Rhondda those days was not very safe for Socialists or Suffragettes. I remember on one occasion two prominent Suffragettes came to address the I.L.P.

The meeting was held in a café on the main street. The local young Liberals League crowded outside shouting slogans and throwing rotten fruit and stones. They smashed the window, the meeting had to be closed, and the Suffragettes had to make an escape down a ladder to the riverside and walk to catch a train at the next station to avoid the mob!

This seems hardly credible these days in Labour's stronghold. The fights in local elections were bitter, but things were so different then. Miners were chosen as candidates and had to fight Colliery Agents, businessmen and property owners. Often our comrades turned out at 5 a.m. to distribute leaflets to the miners as they went to work. But we won victory after victory. Labour gained power and has ruled the Rhondda Council now for many years. Since April 1955 Rhondda has been a Borough. The Council has 44 members. Labour has all the seats but a few.

Chapter Three
Votes for Women

THE FIGHT of women for political freedom is a very inspiring story : inspiring because of the courage of the few women in the early days who had to fight centuries of tradition and prejudice. We women today owe them a great debt of gratitude.

Mary Wollstonecraft in 1792 started the demand for liberty for women. The torch she lit was never extinguished and Adult Suffrage was secured in 1928. It took 136 years to win this freedom for women.

Women who joined organisations in those days were abused. In 1813 Elizabeth Fry, who publicly worked for Prison Reform, shocked those who believed that woman's place was the home, and that no 'good woman' had duties outside its walls.

The novels written by the Brontës and a Queen on the throne all helped in the march of progress. Florence Nightingale, who pioneered the nursing profession in the Crimean War, was called 'A Witch'. Today she is known as 'The Lady with the Lamp'.

Disraeli in 1848 pleaded for political freedom for women. John Bright championed the cause of women in the House, and John Stuart Mill by his books '*Liberty*' (1859) and '*Subjection of Women*' (1869), did much to arouse public interest.

In 1881, when the Franchise Bill was before the House of Commons, one of the Government Ministers who voted against it declared in his speech that 'the *opinion of men was valuable in politics because they were able – one and all – to contribute something of a peculiar and particular knowledge of Law, Trade and Commerce, Armies and War*'. Then he asked '*To

any of these subjects can women contribute any experience?'
Cries of 'No!' As each Bill for Adult Suffrage was outvoted or
talked out, the Suffrage Movement grew stronger and became
more violent in its demands. After the defeat of the 1878
Bill the Suffrage Movement held 1,400 public meetings and
9,563 petitions with 2,953,848 signatures were presented to
Parliament. Up to 1911, twenty-one debates had taken place
and seven Bills had passed the second reading.

Under the Liberal Government – from 1906 to 1914 – five
Suffrage Bills were defeated and this made the Suffragettes
hostile and rebellious. Mr. Asquith, the Prime Minister,
was against Women's Suffrage, but Mr. Lloyd George who
followed him as Premier, made promises of support. When
he did not carry them out, the Suffragettes followed him to
his meetings in Wales, and even to his own constituency in
Caernarvonshire.

Because of the part women played in the First World War,
and as a result of continued agitation, the Government made
some concession in 1918 and granted women over thirty the
vote. But there were certain qualifications – they had to be
married, or if single, had to occupy two rooms and own their
own furniture.

These qualifications denied many women their rights as
citizens. The women were very indignant and the demand for
Adult Suffrage continued. Finally in 1928, the Act was passed
giving votes to men and women at twenty-one years of age.

'Votes for Flappers' was the flippant retort, but in June 1928,
this Act received the Royal assent. The veteran Suffrage leader,
Dame Millicent Fawcett, wrote to Mr. Ramsay MacDonald,
the Leader of the Labour Party, thanking him for the great help
and support the Party had given to the women's cause. It was a
great gain, she said, when one of the Parties adopted the cause
and made it their own.

The Labour Party at their first Conference had placed Adult
Suffrage on their programme and consistently, inside and

outside Parliament, fought for votes for men and women at the age of twenty-one. All our Labour pioneers were great fighters for the political freedom of women.

In my propaganda work I used to quote the following poem, which conveyed in a few words the power of the Vote –

> 'We have a weapon firmer set
> And better than the bayonet ;
> A weapon that comes down as still
> As snowflakes fall upon the grass ;
> Yet, executes the Freeman's will
> As lightning does the Will of God ;
> And from its force – no bolts or bars
> Can shield us – It's *The Ballot Box'.*

This is only a brief history of the fight for the Vote and for woman's equality as citizens, but it is well to remind the younger generation of women of the hard-won freedom they enjoy today.

The Vote broke down age-long barriers to women in all the professions. It opened the door for women to enter Parliament, local and national councils, law, medicine, industry, religion and all social work. Old customs were overthrown. No longer could the men persuade us that women were their intellectual inferiors.

The marriage bar has almost been removed in all professions. The old idea that home and child-bearing was woman's chief function in life has gone. Nevertheless to the majority of women, homemaking will still remain their chief and noblest contribution in life, for home is not only a place to eat and sleep in, it is the abiding place of the family where the character of our future citizens is made or marred.

But there are women who, by training and ability, can make a valuable contribution outside the home. To deny women this opportunity, or deny her marriage and family as well, is denying her the freedom we have fought for.

We were told when agitating for the Vote – often very patronisingly by men – that woman's place was to fit the child for the world. We retorted that if it was woman's place to fit the child for the world, it was also her place to fit the world for the child, and before we could do either, we must take an interest in politics.

In the last war, Hitler drove the German women back to the kitchen. That was the beginning of the end of Germany. It is the 'writing on the wall' for all other nations to heed. *No nation grows faster than its women.* The Vote is now our birthright. Let us treasure it, and guard against any temptation to sell it for 'a mess of pottage' at Election times.

Chapter Four
Women in the Labour Party

THE LABOUR Party up to 1918 was chiefly composed of Trade Unions and a few Socialist organisations. When Adult Suffrage was won it meant that the Party had to revise its constitution to allow two types of membership ; affiliated and individual membership. This was done at the Party conference at Nottingham in January 1918.

Some of our leading women had been active in the Women's Labour League, Independent Labour Party, Fabian Society, Co-operative Women's Guilds and Suffrage organisations.

So in 1918, the Women's Labour League (formed in 1906) was merged into the Labour Party constitution and became the forerunner of our Women's Sections. Dr. Marion Phillips, who was its Secretary, became the first Chief Woman Officer of the Party.

To organise the new woman voter into the Labour Party, a women's department was set up and women organisers appointed. I was the fourth and started my work in March 1919. My territory then went beyond the bounds of Wales. Travelling was not easy, there were no bus services as there are today, trains were few and far between and not very comfortable. Neither was hotel accommodation very good in many towns. I spent the first week of my appointment at Head Office with Dr. Marion Phillips, and one of my first jobs was to translate two English leaflets into the Welsh language for women voters. This was to help organise women in North and Mid-Wales.

Early in my appointment I was called upon to help some of our speakers with propaganda. I addressed meetings in the

South of England. Very hostile questions were asked about the miners and the mining industry, for at that time the South Wales Miners' Federation was taking a lead in Labour politics. All Socialists were thought to be atheists and anti-Christian. I remember well a challenge we had on Boscombe Pier at one of our meetings from a member of the Plymouth Brethren Movement. He challenged us to prayer. This challenge was accepted by the Rev. Fred Hopkins, one of our propagandists. After he had prayed he asked the challenger to pray. The meeting was taken by surprise – it had a wonderful effect on the crowd and our speakers had a good hearing.

My first by-election was at Swansea East in 1919. Alderman David Williams, J.P., was our candidate, Mr. Egerton Wake from Head Office acted as Agent. Our Candidate was a great worker on the Council. Swansea at that time was a Liberal stronghold. We were unsuccessful, but polled well. Mrs. David Williams was one of our first Magistrates, one of the first members of the Labour Women's League in Swansea and a member of the Co-operative Guild Central Committee. She did much good work for Maternity and Child Welfare in the town. She helped us greatly in the early days to organise the women into the Party. We cherished her wise guidance and loyalty. The silver cup she presented to us for the annual competition among the Sections keeps her memory ever green in the minds of Labour women. Both she and her husband were great workers for the I.L.P.

My second by-election was in the Wrekin Division of Shropshire in 1920, when Charles Duncan, General Secretary of the Workers Union was the candidate. It was a very interesting election as we were fighting one of Horatio Bottomley's so-called Independent candidates. It was more like a circus than an election. Our opponents had a number of sandwich board men carrying huge posters round and round in the square in Wellington, the main market town.

In 1920 the Party divided the country into seven regions for

organising work. A man and a woman organiser were appointed
for each region. Mr. T.C. Morris became my colleague and
we were given the whole of Wales as our territory. When I
commenced my work I had very little equipment: just a bundle
of index cards with the addresses of Trade Unions Secretaries,
a report book and some leaflets. But I and my other colleagues
launched out on this work with a deep conviction and
missionary zeal, preaching this new gospel of Socialism and
prepared to meet all opposition and difficulties. All our work
had to be done from our own homes. I soon learnt typing and
duplicating which was essential.

In 1919 there were three branches of the Women's Labour
League in South Wales, at Cardiff, Swansea and Newport.
They became the forerunners of our Women's Organisation
and helped to organise the first Women's Conferences. The
first was at Pontypridd in 1918, and others followed at Cardiff,
Swansea and Newport. Dr. Marion Phillips was the speaker
at each. So the foundation was laid for Advisory Councils to
cover eventually the whole of Wales.

The setting up of the Councils gave scope to venture out on
new methods of educating the women in politics. The Labour
League members became our first Officers. Much work was
done by these first Advisory Councils to help to organise
sections in each Parliamentary Division. As the sections grew
in number on a Ward basis, we had to set up some co-ordinating
body inside the Divisions, so Central Committees of officers
of Women's Sections were formed in Borough Divisions, and
Federations of Women's Sections in County Divisions.

As the movement grew we found that we had to co-ordinate
the work of the Advisory Councils, so as to take united part
in campaigns and any other work which the Standing Joint
Committee of Industrial Women's Organisations called upon
us to do. So the Joint Advisory Committee was set up to
organise summer schools, annual conferences and rallies and
soon our first joint conference was held at Cory Hall, Cardiff

in September 1938.

War in 1939 made it impossible to hold our conference that year, but we ventured to call a conference in 1940 and have continued it annually ever since.

The 1945 conference at Cory Hall, Cardiff will be long remembered. The General Election had been declared, so we gave up our afternoon session to co-operate with the Regional Council of Labour in an Election meeting to open the campaign in Wales.

It was a great gathering: Mr. Clem Attlee our Leader, and Mr. James Griffiths, M.P., were our speakers. They were received with great enthusiasm.

Labour won this Election with a good majority, and thus an opportunity came to lay the foundation for the Welfare State that Keir Hardie and other pioneers had visualised. During Labour's term in power, revolutionary changes were made in our social services and in the economic life of the nation.

The next phase will be realised when we return another Labour Government with a good majority. Socialism is dynamic; if it remains static we shall lose all that we have gained. In the words of one of our pioneers –'We march on! I see a horizon: I want my children to see a further horizon – and their children to see further horizons still'.

This is the Socialist way to Progress.

Chapter Five
Towards New Horizons

IN THE early days, women were very new in politics, and were afraid of being called Suffragettes. Much educational work had to be done in simple language, and made interesting.

Realising this, I decided to interest them by charts, and the first one I drafted was 'Mother in the Home' surrounded by all the laws that affected her in every aspect of daily life.

This chart became very popular and I realised that visual aid was to play an important part in my propaganda work. Our Socialist propaganda had to have a sense of reality. We were not only a political Party, but a great Movement, concerned about human personalities and their well-being.

Effective propaganda work on Labour's policy was done by means of attractive tableaux and pageantry at our special rallies and 'Women's Months'. One outstanding procession was in Swansea. Sir Alfred Mond, its M.P., was Minister of Health and his plea for economy by cutting down on milk for babies and housing had aroused the women of the country. Our West Wales Advisory Committee organised a procession through the town with meetings in the Park. The band we had engaged failed us, so we had a silent procession carrying banners with slogans like these –

'LABOUR WOMEN SAY MOND MUST GO'
'STINT THE MILK AND STARVE THE CHILD'

It was interesting to see the public reading these banners as we passed by. *At the next Election Mond did go and we won this seat for Labour for the first time!*

The first Women's Section was formed at Ton Pentre, Rhondda in 1918 with the help of the local Trades Council. I was appointed Secretary. There were twelve women present. At that time the South Wales Miners' Federation were agitating for shorter hours and higher wages. When discussing this matter, the women felt that the time was long overdue to get something done to lighten the burden of the miner's wife.

I wrote a letter to the Miners' conference saying we wholeheartedly supported their demands and while doing so, thought the time had come when shorter hours for miners' wives should have some consideration. We also made the request that the question of pit baths should be a part of their campaign. This letter was read to the conference and interest was aroused as well as some opposition. The Press gave this matter much publicity and I had many lively discussions with some of the miners' leaders.

On pit baths, Katherine Bruce Glasier had already done much propaganda work with the Women's Labour League. A pamphlet was written jointly by Katherine, Robert Smillie (President of the Miners' Federation of Great Britain) and G.R. Carter, M.A., which had photographs of pit baths that had been built at a British colliery and in France and Belgium. Katherine had made arrangements to meet the miners' leaders at the 1913 Trade Union Congress to discuss this question. She was aroused to immense indignation when one of them from Wales tore up the pamphlet, threw it away and called her a 'dreamer'. *This pamphlet eventually ran into six editions and was endorsed by the Miners' Federation of Great Britain itself!*

She was delighted when I took up this campaign and gave evidence before the Sankey Commission in 1919 on pit baths and housing, on behalf of the South Wales Miners' Federation. A great bond of friendship arose between us that lasted until the end of her days in 1950.

In South Wales, the Ocean Colliery Company, with the personal interest of the two Misses Davies of Llandinam, gave the movement an impetus, and the first pit baths were built at

Treharris. In 1919 I arranged for the Ton Pentre Section and the Co-operative Guild to visit these baths. Many other parties from the coalfield sponsored by the miners' lodges followed, and thus the campaign went on.

In addition, I had the load of lantern slides on pit baths from the Welsh Housing Association whose secretary, Mr. Edgar Chappell, was keenly interested in the campaign. I was able to get the use of Workmen's Halls to show these slides, and with the help of the Miners' political organisers carried this campaign to all the mining areas of South Wales.

In many a cottage there were three or four miners having to bath in a tub in front of the fire. The small kitchen was often the only available living room in the house and had to serve as bathroom, laundry, bakery, dining room and nursery. The heat from the large open fire, and the stench from the wet pit clothes made the atmosphere unbearable. The mother and wife had to tolerate all this.

But still amongst the miners and their families, prejudices had to be overcome, old ideas destroyed and convincing facts marshalled to prove the benefit of pit baths.

The Royal Commission on the Mining Industry – generally known from its chairman as the Sankey Commission – was set up in 1918. Dr. Marion Phillips suggested that women from the mining areas should give evidence on housing and pit baths. I was asked by the South Wales Miners' Federation to represent South Wales. Mrs. Hart came from Wigan, and Mrs. Brown from Scotland. We three gave evidence.

When we arrived in London we were besieged by the Press at the hotel, and during the time we were giving evidence we were photographed and a minute description given of our dresses.

Many of the personal remarks amused us greatly. They expected us to be overawed at being in the King's Robing Room in the House of Lords where the Commission was held. They also expressed surprise at our calmness when giving evidence.

I dealt with the overcrowding in the mining areas of South Wales and the strain on the miner's wife from lifting of tubs and heavy boilers. This accounted for the high maternal mortality. The drying of pit clothes in an overcrowded kitchen played havoc with the health of young children. The infant mortality rate in the Rhondda was 105 per 1,000.

The proposals put forward in the Sankey Commission Report included better housing, pit head baths and holidays with pay. All these were shelved for many years and the position in the coalfield grew steadily worse. From 1921 to 1932, 250,000 people left South Wales to look for work elsewhere. The aftermath of the 1914-18 War had a disastrous effect on the coal industry in this country. Mass unemployment and the family Means Test drove many young members of the families away from home. Those that remained, unable to find jobs, expressed themselves by mass demonstrations, protest meetings and deputations.

Then came the General Strike and Lock-out from May to December 1926. It was during this period of poverty and distress that Communist propaganda had a good following in the Rhondda, and the township of Mardy became named 'Little Moscow'. The Communists captured the Executive of the Rhondda Borough Party which had to be disaffiliated and reorganised. We Labour people suffered much from their attacks, which were often very personal.

Today their strength has faded. A better standard of life, and better conditions for the workers are the only answer to Communist propaganda. Our experience in the Rhondda is a miniature lesson for the undeveloped countries. Poverty and injustice must be removed.

Chapter Six
The Walls of Jericho

NORTH WALES was a special problem for organisation. The Non-conformist Churches had a tremendous grip over the people and were the centre of all their activities. The women were not accustomed to political and industrial struggles and were shy of taking part in meetings.

But our propaganda in North Wales did much to bring North and South Wales nearer to each other. In the early days, the South Walians were looked upon as rebels, and there was a prevalent idea that if any Northman did wrong, he found a refuge in South Wales, especially in the Rhondda. '*Lawr i'r gweithiau yn y De'.* (Gone down to the works in South Wales') was the saying.

Invariably at my meetings someone would tell me they had been working in the Rhondda Valley. They were our keen supporters in the North Wales villages, and made considerable sacrifices to organise Labour meetings.

Dr. Marion Phillips paid many visits to North Wales as Chief Woman Officer, and from 1932 Miss Mary Sutherland was always welcome by our Labour women.

We tried to get publicity for our work in the local Press, and I was able to get several articles, in the Welsh language, into the weekly Welsh Labour Paper 'Y Dinesydd' ('The Citizen'), on social problems affecting women and children. Unfortunately this paper only had a short life.

To fight Liberalism in Wales was much more difficult than fighting Toryism. The Liberals were much more bitter towards us. Churches and Chapels were the centre of their activities and Socialism was believed to be an anti-Christian movement.

In our propaganda we said Socialism was the only way to put our Christian principles into practice in everyday life.

North Wales had always been the stronghold of Liberalism. The influence of the two Welsh Prime Ministers and their families – Ewart Gladstone at Hawarden, Flintshire, and Lloyd George in Caernarvon – had a great effect on North Wales politics. It was like confronting the Walls of Jericho to attack these Liberal strongholds. Labour trumpets had to be blown very hard and very often! However, with patience and the help of devoted comrades, the walls of Liberalism gave way one by one.

I treasure the help I had in those difficult days. Mrs. Silyn Roberts of Bangor gave me much encouragement. She was for many years Secretary of the North Wales' Workers' Educational Association, and in that sphere has a noble record. She took over this work when her husband, Rev. Silyn Roberts, passed away. He had been Secretary and Lecturer for the W.E.A. and extra-mural classes of the University in North Wales for many years. His influence still remains in the life of the quarrymen of North Wales. He was a great lecturer, a noble character, and much beloved by his people. I owe them both very much for the inspiration they gave me. Alderman H.T. Edwards, Shotton, was another great comrade who worked to build up the organisation in North Wales.

I had to find many ways of getting meetings organised. I well remember my first meeting in Flintshire, addressing the Deeside Trades Council at Shotton. The Secretary was a great worker in the Brotherhood Movement, and he arranged for me to visit the Brotherhood. A Minister from a Church in Queensferry was present and he in turn asked me to the Sisterhood at his Church. The Trades Council also organised a meeting for me at the village hall, Hawarden, the home of the Gladstone family. It was the first Labour meeting ever held there and twelve people came.

The death of Arthur Deakin in 1955 was a great loss to

our Movement. Before he was elected as General Secretary of the Transport Workers' Union, he had spent many years in Shotton as the Union's North Wales Secretary. In this capacity he gave me much help in Flintshire. Alderman H.T. Edwards who followed him also gave me invaluable aid.

Along the coastline from Chester to Llandudno there has been a great migration of people from Liverpool, Manchester and Lancashire, so the English language predominates. But further North and inland in Flintshire, the Welsh language is strong. This created some difficulty for me, because Welsh in North Wales is much more guttural than in the South. I found a way out by keeping to 'Bible Welsh' which both North and South understands!

David Lloyd George was then the M.P. for Caernarvon Borough, and I took part in the 1924 Election when Professor Simmon fought him for Labour. At that time it was woe betide anyone who said anything about Lloyd George or even mentioned his name on our platform. There was an outbreak of clapping and booing and meetings became pandemonium. Lloyd George got in of course, but we had carried our message into the Liberal citadel.

We had great times in by-elections even though we were storming Liberal strongholds. In Anglesey in 1923 we had a lot of trouble in one part of the town with the children. They would flock to the front seats at our meetings, and as soon as they started, clap and chant 'R.J. is a gentleman'. 'R.J.' was the Liberal Candidate and a very popular businessman in Holyhead. We had to turn the children out before our speakers got a chance.

Of all problems in North Wales, the worst was tuberculosis. The death rate was terrible and we knew that social conditions were at the root of the problem. In 1933, the Welsh National Memorial Association conducted an investigation into it.

Dr. Herbert Chalke's report revealed some astounding facts about improper and inadequate diet, overcrowding, bad housing, poor sanitation, impaired general health, and fatigue and exposure. Caernarvonshire, for instance, had the highest tuberculosis rate in Wales. In one of its districts, Gwyrfai, the rate was double that of the whole county. Merioneth too, had a high incidence.

After this report, the Labour Women's Advisory Council started an intensive campaign to see if Dr. Chalke's findings could be put into effect by the Local Authorities. He had suggested cleaner milk and water supplies, replacing damp cottages, better sanitation, provision of facilities for drying clothes in schools and quarries, the development of village institutes, healthy indoor and outdoor recreation, school meals and canteens at the quarries. Dr. Chalke recommended that all organisations should enlist in a 'better health' propaganda campaign, particularly directed to mothers and children.

The report gave our Labour women the facts necessary to arouse the women of the area to their responsibility. Conferences and public meetings were organised and resolutions passed and sent on to the local authorities. We were called 'a lot of interfering women' for telling the Councils what they ought to do.

In 1939 there was yet another report by Dr. Coutts and Mr. Clement Davies, M.P. for Montgomeryshire, that shocked us all. Seven of our Welsh Counties were the highest on the mortality black list for tuberculosis. So the campaign went on to arouse public opinion and slow-moving local authorities to a sense of responsibility.

The latest figures show a remarkable decline. In 1913 there were 1,269 deaths from T.B. in Wales, in 1953 only 278. The waiting list for admission to hospital is much reduced. The introduction of the National Health Service by the Labour Government, and the higher standard of living of our people has given us hope that some day this scourge will be a thing of the past. For T.B. fundamentally is a disease with social causes, and like many others which have haunted humanity in bygone days, can be wiped out if we have the means and the will. Today we are seeing the reward of our efforts of a quarter of a century ago. We still need 'interfering women' to carry them on!

Chapter Seven
1926 and After

THE MINERS' Lock-out following the General Strike will ever be remembered in the mining valleys of Wales. Our Women's Organisations were faced with a tremendous responsibility in mitigating the distress caused by this terrible industrial struggle, in which they stood loyally by their menfolk in the fight for better conditions.

Our Advisory Councils worked with the Relief Committee of the Standing Joint Committee of Industrial Women's Organisations, of which Dr. Marion Phillips was Secretary. Mrs. Ayrton Gould, Chairman, and Lady Slesser, Treasurer. Under the guidance of these three great women, we set up in Wales in a very short time a wonderful network of organisations to look after expectant and nursing mothers, children and sick people.

Parcels of food, medical supplies, and clothing were given to those in need. Sewing Committees were set up and for these we bought material from money received as discount and dividend on purchases. The private traders as well as our Co-operative Societies were very generous. We made maternity outfits, baby garments, and children's clothes, as well as adult clothing. We cut up old clothing from parcels sent to us, and made thousands of garments in this way. Boot repairing centres were established; our men worked voluntarily and thousands of our people were kept shod as a result. We received in Wales nearly £21,000 from the Relief Committee's Central Fund, which became known as the 'Slesser Fund'.

Besides hundreds of parcels and sacks of clothing, we received boxes of condensed milk, cocoa and baby food and also large cases of footwear from the Boot and Shoe Operatives' Trade Union. Parcels came from Denmark, Norway, Sweden, Germany, Canada, Australia and other countries. In London, Dr. Marion Phillips organised an adoption scheme so that friends could look after a miner's child for the period of the Lock-out. Over 800 children came from Wales, selected from the largest families in greatest need. We arranged with the railway company to take parties of forty to fifty children to London each week. A few were adopted in Birmingham and Swindon.

Our Sewing Committees saw to it that each child was clothed decently so as not to be an object of pity on arrival. The hostesses met them at Paddington and took them to their homes.

At first parents were not very willing to let the children go, but once the first party wrote home to say what lovely homes they had, we could hardly cope with the demand. One little girl from a very poor home gave a description of her lovely bedroom overlooking a flower garden. She said it made her think that she was in Heaven. The railway company made generous concessions in fares and provided a special coach on the London train for these parties. Mrs. Beatrice Green, of Abertillery, well known for her ability as a speaker, addressed meetings in London to raise funds for the Committee. One incident made a lasting impression on her mind. It was an open-air meeting in a thickly-populated district. In the audience was a little ragged boy. He came near, tugged at her frock and said: 'I ain't got a penny miss, but I will sing for you'. He sang a popular song with such feeling that it carried away the meeting and the money thrown into the circle made a record collection. Mrs. Johanna James, Tonypandy, and Mrs. Herman, Pentre, also addressed meetings in London. The three were miner's wives and good speakers.

The Welsh children returning after the settlement of the Lock-out were so loaded with presents for themselves and families, that we had to reserve two compartments for gifts only. Some of them had forgotten the name of their home towns and it took me all my time to sort them out. Lasting friendships were formed between the children, their parents and their hosts, who were by now 'Aunts and Uncles' to them all. Many a motherless child found a permanent home.

I have always believed that environment is an important factor in the life of a child. This experiment proved it beyond doubt, as well as the old saying – *'It is an ill wind that blows no one any good'.*

During all these months our people never lost hope. They kept busy with soup kitchens, concerts, jazz bands, competitive meetings, and many other activities. Much latent talent was found among our young people through these efforts.

Of the many friends and organisations which came to our aid, I must mention two that gave great help, not only financially, but socially, morally and spiritually.

The Society of Friends sent Mr. and Mrs. Noble to Rhondda, where they organised groups of men and women to help themselves. The unemployed built huts in many parts of the valley to carry on the work financed by the Friends. Men repaired boots and shoes, and dressmaking was done by the women. In a very short time there were fifty-two men's groups and twenty women's groups in the area.

The Society of Friends then took over a big house called 'Maes-yr-haf', Trealaw. In the spring of 1927 it was opened as a Centre for educational and cultural activities. Mr. and Mrs. Noble became the first Wardens. They both entered into the life and problems of the Valley with great sympathy and understanding.

'Maes-yr-haf' is still with us and very active in the life of the community under the guidance of the Wardens, Mr. and Mrs. F. B. Naylor.

Another Centre that came to our aid in those difficult years of mass unemployment was the 'House of Trees', Williamstown,

Rhondda, which was taken over by the Salvation Army Goodwill organisation. Under the guidance of Major and Mrs. Markham, helped by Hugh Redwood (author of *'God in the slums'*), this Centre became very active in the Rhondda. At that time eight out of every ten men were unemployed.

The house, with many outbuildings and acres of mountain land around it, was turned into an Occupational Centre to help young people. The land was tilled and workshops opened, finding employment for between fifty and sixty youths. Up to March 1939, 1,400 youths had been helped at this Centre.

In 1942 the Home Office took over the 'House of Trees' as a probation Hostel run jointly with the Salvation Army, so its good work still continues.

Young delinquents are sent there for training and supervision. They learn farming, poultry-keeping, woodwork, and gardening. Many a young lad with a sad home-life and upbringing has found a real home atmosphere at this Hostel. Some have settled down in the neighbourhood, others gone farming in this country and overseas, but they all keep in touch with the 'House of Trees', remembering the loving care, understanding and help they received there.

During the depression I was asked to lecture to a very distinguished gathering on the effect of mass unemployment on the lives of women. After stating many facts, I said that their feelings could be best summed up in this poem:

> 'Nid cardod I ddyn-ond gwaith,
> Mae dyn rhy fawr I gardod.
> Mae cardod yn magu craeth,
> A craeth yn magu nychdod'.

The translation in English is:

> 'Not charity for men, but work:
> Man is too big for charity.

Charity leaves a scar,
And a scar becomes a festering sore'.

Keir Hardie in his maiden speech in the House of Commons in 1906, speaking for the unemployed of those days, said 'One of the most harrowing features connected with the problem of the unemployed is not the poverty or hardship they have to endure, but the fearful moral degradation that follows in the wake of enforced idleness, and there is no more pitiable spectacle in the world than the man willing to work who, day by day, vainly begs a brother of the earth to give him leave to toil'.

How true is this! When history comes to be written about the period of mass unemployment it will be dealt with in statistics and percentages. Readers and students of the future will need much imagination and understanding to give the human factor its rightful place. I hope what I have written will help.

Chapter Eight
Mothers and Babies

DURING THE greater part of the nineteenth century, every constructive effort to relieve poverty and distress was made by voluntary bodies in this country. Pawnshops and lodging-houses and Poor Law dominated the lives of very poor people. Local Government was restricted to Public Health Acts and the Poor Law Act of 1834.

The Standing Joint Committee of Industrial Women's Organisations, set up with representatives from the Women's Labour League, Trade Unions, and the Co-operative Guild, did much to inspire women on social problems.

The campaign on maternity and child welfare is a story on its own, and has to be told so that women of today can appreciate the work that was done in the early days for the care of mother and child.

In England before 1900, despite medical opinion, a large number of women were practising as midwives who were ignorant, ill-trained, and only tolerated because there was no other provision.

When a child was expected into a working class home, it was taken for granted that a friendly neighbour or relation would take the responsibility. No training was considered necessary, and where no-one was available to do the job for love, they hired a handy woman who, Charles Dickens describes as '*The Sairey Gamp who was as equally good at a lying-in, as at a laying-out*'.

After years of struggle by women who realised the waste of life and untold suffering among mothers as consequence of untrained women attending them at childbirth, Parliament in

1902 passed the first Midwives Act and sought to remedy this by setting up a Register of those who had passed an examination after training. The standard was very low at first. As soon as the Register was established a large number of women took the training and earned their livelihood as midwives. At first the fee was as low as 5/-. The trained midwives then founded the Midwives Institute to work for improvements in nursing and better training.

We have travelled far since then. Today we have a well-trained municipal service of midwives, which is the basis of a good maternity service.

The Women's Labour League Conference, held in London in 1912, was a real landmark in the agitation for the welfare of mothers and children.

Miss Margaret Llewellyn Davies, the General Secretary of the Co-operative Women's Guild, brought out a book in 1915 called '*Maternity*'. It comprised letters from working women written in answer to an enquiry into conditions of motherhood by Guild members.

In a preface, Sir Herbert Samuel (now Lord Samuel), who was President of the Local Government Board, wrote:

> '*We have facts which have hitherto been hidden. It is the first time that these have been stated, not by medical men or social students, but by the sufferers themselves. It is necessary to take action to solve the problems that here stand revealed*'.

This book gave women impetus for a rousing campaign, and every opportunity was seized to bring this problem to the forefront. Much work had to be done to educate public opinion and local authorities.

There was a feeling prevalent that it is not very respectable for speakers to discuss maternal mortality and maternal morbidity in public meetings. I met with this attitude myself as a Guild speaker, but I soon found out that our menfolk were very sympathetic. It was a sad home when the mother died or was maimed in health. Many a sad story I heard from mothers in those early days who were suffering as a result of neglect during childbirth. I could speak with some feeling on this matter for ten of our family were born before 1900 under the 'handy women' regime.

Between 1891 and 1900 there was an average of 140,000 infant deaths each year. From 1910 to 1922 the death rate of mothers in the Rhondda was the third highest for the country due to lack of housing and hospitals where serious and abnormal cases could be dealt with. The incidence of death from sepsis, more commonly known as 'bed fever,' was very high. The miner's wife in those days ran greater risks at childbirth that her man in the pit.

In 1924 Dame Janet M. Campbell, M.D., Senior Medical Officer to Sir George Newman, Chief Medical Officer, submitted her third report on her inquiry into maternal mortality. This is a quotation:

> *'There are no less than* 700,000 *mothers in England and Wales giving birth to children per annum. Of this number approximately* 3,000 *have died during the last ten years in the fulfilment of this maternal function. This is a serious and largely an avoidable loss of life. Yet the number of deaths by no means indicates the whole loss, for a vastly greater number than* 3,000 *were permanently injured or invalided in childbirth.'*

This report was submitted to the Minister of Health in 1924 and gives us a vivid picture of the loss of life among mothers. Three counties in Wales — Breconshire, Montgomeryshire and Pembrokeshire — were quoted for a very high maternal and infantile mortality.

In 1927 Dame Janet Campbell made another report on

the Protection of Motherhood. These reports aroused the public and local authorities to a sense of responsibility to the motherhood of the nation.

Our Labour Women's organisations seized every opportunity to get these facts across, and to arouse public authorities to make full use of their powers.

The 1918 Maternity Act made it compulsory on local authorities to set up Maternity and Child Welfare Clinics, but as with all reforms, much work had to be done to convince mothers of their value. Many ghosts had to be laid — false modesty, ignorance, and the old-fashioned idea that mothers knew all about motherhood by instinct, and needed no advice.

The Rhondda Council was ready to adopt any new proposals from the Government on Maternity and Child Welfare, and so led the way. The 1918 Act suggested that Councils should co-opt two women representing women's organisations on Maternity and Child Welfare Committees. There were no women councillors in those days. We campaigned in all the counties of Wales urging local authorities to do this and get on with this important work.

We were very surprised at the attitude of many County Medical Officers of Health when we made this request. Our letters were quite courteous and business like, but one County M.O.H referred to them as '*wild hysterical effusions*' and falling back on scriptural phraseology, said the Council must be charitable to such people '*as they know not what they are talking about*'. In another county we were called a '*lot of interfering busybodies*'.

The Standing Joint Committee of Industrial Women's Organisation did great work on problems affecting women and children. When the Labour Party set up the Women's Department in 1918, Dr. Phillips, as Chief Woman Officer, was able to give our Sections and Advisory Councils wise guidance in their campaign.

We went forth with our requests to local authorities for a municipal service of Midwives, Health Visitors, Maternity and Child Welfare Clinics, Home Helps and special food for expectant and nursing mothers, and in the rural areas for travelling Maternity Clinics and telephone kiosks in every village to give access to nurse and doctor.

Alderman Rose Davies, C.B.E., J.P., of Aberdare represented the Labour women of Wales on the Standing Joint Committee for over twenty-five years and during those years she kept our Advisory Councils, Women's Conferences, and Sections well informed and gave great help in this campaign. Rose was the first woman on the Glamorgan County Council, was appointed Alderman and became the first Woman Chairman of the Council. She has done invaluable work on the welfare of mother and child. She was one of the first members of the Independent Labour Party at Aberdare and came under the influence of Keir Hardie, who had been a guest in her home. We have both enjoyed a long friendship.

In 1918 we were appointed to the Consultative Council for the Ministry of Health for Wales, and submitted a joint memorandum on Maternity and Child Welfare work.

We have been spared to see the results of the campaign in the reduction of maternal and infantile mortality and greater care of expectant and nursing mothers in Wales. Precious lives have been saved, mothers are healthier and babies are bonnier, but there is still much work to be done.

Chapter Nine
The Children That Will Be

THE STORY of the Nursery School movement is one of the most romantic of our time. The campaign for the establishment of Nursery Schools has gone on steadily since 1816 when Robert Owen opened a school at New Lanark where children from the age of two were cared for while their mothers worked in the mils.

But it is to later pioneers like Margaret McMillan and her sister Rachel that the movement owes its inspiration and acceptance in the education system of our country.

Visiting Bradford to lecture in 1893, Margaret and Rachel had found themselves among men and women whom they recognised as natural comrades, like Katherine and Bruce Glasier, F.W. Jowett, Keir Heidie, Enid Stacey and many other notable pioneers who had formed the first branch of the Independent Labour Party.

So Margaret remained in Bradford, was elected to the School Board, and thus began her life's work for children. She addressed meetings for the I.L.P. all over the country and wrote pamphlets and articles for the Press. Due to her pioneering work and inspiration we now have school clinics, school doctors, school baths, school dentistry, school meals, open-air schools, and nursery schools.

She really was a wonderful person, a dynamic personality with a purpose and mission in life. '*All children are mine*' was her motto.

Her work in the Socialist Movement was the means by which Labour became the greatest force for education amongst all political parties. She introduced a new and splendid realism.

Parliament began to take notice of her work and in 1907 passed a small Act — The Education (Administrative Provisions) Act — which was the first of a series that have changed the whole face of British education.

In Bradford she found appalling conditions amongst school children. The 'half timers' slept exhausted at their desks and children from the streets and alleys were in every stage of physical misery. She set to work to bring about a series of reforms through the School Board and helped to make Bradford the leading city in educational progress. Robert Blatchford said of her that she was a '*blend of Joan of Arc and Florence Nightingale, tempered with the humour of Jane Austen*'.

In 1910 Margaret and her sister Rachel started the first Nursery School at Deptford, London, in a poor and thickly populated district. In 1917 Rachel died, so Margaret was left to carry on the work with a small staff. The sisters were very devoted to each other and their work.

The Annual Reports of Sir George Newman, Chief Medical Officer of Health, did much to arouse the conscience of the nation to the appalling neglect of the pre-school child. He revealed in one of his reports that of two million toddlers between two and five years of age, 31 per cent. were dull or very dull through preventable causes, and one million children became 'Damaged goods' before they reached the age of five. The School medical service had to spend most of its time and energy in patching them up.

The Maternity and Child Welfare Act of 1918 provided for the health of babies up to two, and at five the school authorities stepped in, but the damage was done to the child's health between these ages. Nursery schools were needed to fill this gap.

During Margaret McMillan's visits to Wales I was privileged to entertain her in my home. While discussing the possibility of getting Nursery schools in the Rhondda she visualised the

day when they would be built on the hillsides and she wrote
this poem:

> '*The mountains and the little hills*
> *Will laugh with joy one day,*
> *When troop on troop of little bairns*
> *Will make their summit gay,*
> *And down the sunlit shadowy sides*
> *The pitmen's eyes will see*
> *The fairest flowers of all the Vale,*
> *That ever glowed on hill or dale,*
> *The children that will be'.*

In September 1935, ten years after she wrote this poem, the
first Nursery School was opened on the hillside at Ynyscynon,
Llwnpia, Rhondda, for 120 children. At their first Christmas
party I presented the school with an illuminated copy of her
poem, the original manuscript and a photograph of her. It is
greatly treasured.

It will be a happy day for mothers and little toddlers when
nursery schools become an integral part of our educational
system as maternity and child welfare is part of our Health
Services.

In 1931 our Advisory Councils carried on an intensive
campaign on nursery schools. We met several Labour groups
on Councils to press them to work for one nursery school to
be established in each education area. We women felt that if
this could be done, it would be far more effective to convince
them of this need than passing resolutions. We also got them to
agree to include nursery schools in their Election addresses.

The last time I saw Margaret McMillan in 1931 she was
disappointed, after doing so much propaganda work in Wales,
that we have not produced one nursery school. I made her a
pledge that I would continue to carry on the campaign. Cardiff
opened a nursery school soon after Rhondda and in 1935
Katherine Bruce Glasier opened one at Swansea. Many others

have been opened since.

Since the war the agitation has died down, for day nurseries came to the forefront to help married women to do war work. Nursery classes in the Infant schools have been developed in many areas, but however good these are, they are only substitutes for Nursery schools. It is at the Nursery school that we can find out physical and mental defects and other problems affecting children and get them remedied before they leave for Primary school. Many people still think that a nursery school is just for poor children or a place where mothers can send their children when they go out to work. Margaret McMillan's idea went much deeper. Our propaganda must be revived and continued. Her death in 1931 was a great loss to the nation. She gave forty years of her life to the welfare of little children and her work must go on.

When she died the 'Times' wrote this about her work: *'She developed a rare, intensely impressive and disturbing appeal. Textile workers were made aware of their children not as potential 'doffers' and 'little pieces', but as the heirs of the Ages. Their children were likened to the lilies of the field, and the unfolding of the child mind to the unfolding of creation. Radiant with conviction, she spoke of a light shining above the place where a child lay; she made the earnest souls in the audience see the light. In those missionary days, a speech by Margaret McMillan left groups of her listeners with a vision that for days and weeks kept them quickened and aglow.'*

A memorial has been raised to her memory in the form of a Training College for Nursery School teachers at Bradford, where she blazed the trail. I was glad to take part, with our Labour women and the teaching profession in Wales, in raising money for this memorial. There is another College at Deptford in memory of her sister Rachel.

Her dream can, and must, become a living force in our educational system.

Chapter Ten
The Fight for Pensions

THE STORY of the fight for the care of the aged by the Labour Movement should be told over and over again. It has gone in and out of Parliament since 1889.

Labour propaganda during Elections did much to arouse public opinion on social problems, and by-elections gave us a glorious opportunity to bring this one to the forefront. In 1907 two by-elections were fought and won by Labour candidates on this issue alone: at Jarrow and Colne Valley.

In 1898 a Conference was called in London jointly with the Trade Unions to demand 'Old Age Pensions.' Will Crooks, M.P., George Barnes, M.P., and Margaret Bondfield played a great part in it. Other conferences followed and a National Committee of organised Labour for 'Old Age Pensions' was formed. The T.U.C., the Labour Party and Co-operative Congress actively supported the movement. At first the National Committee's demand was a very modest one. They asked for a non-contributory scheme to provide pensions of not less than 5/-.

In the 1906 General Election, the Liberals were returned with a big majority. Many were pledged to support the demand and the hopes of the aged ran very high. On March 14th, 1906, the Labour Party's motion advocating pensions was approved by the House of Commons, but the Liberal Government did nothing.

Early in 1907 it was known that there would be a surplus on the Budget and the country expected that Old Age Pensions would be included in the Government programme. But the King's speech contained no mention of it. A Labour amendment to the Address, regretting this omission, was defeated by 231 votes to 61. At that time Labour had only thirty M.P's, so it was clear that some of the others supported them.

The result of the two by-elections at Jarrow and Colne Valley was a warning to the Government. In 1908 a Bill was introduced for pensions at seventy years of age instead of sixty-five years, as previously demanded. The rates were 5/- for the husband and 2/6 for the wife. Those on Poor Law relief were to receive nothing. Labour protests were strong enough to induce the Government to concede the full 10/- a week for aged couples, and the ban on Poor Law relief was dropped. The Act came in to operation in January 1909.

In 1919 a special Committee was set up and the majority report recommended 10/- a week without a Means Test. The minority favoured a Means Test and so the minority report was adopted by the Government. This meant any old person with a yearly income of £21 got 5/- and those with an income of £28 17s Gd to £31 got 1/-. Above that there was no pension at all.

The first Labour Government in 1924 (a minority one) effected an improvement to allow pensions to those whose income was £39 a year. As a result 63,000 old people's pensions were increased to full rate and 170,000 obtained pensions for the first time.

In 1925 the Conservative Government passed a Contributory Pensions Act dealing with old people, widows and orphans. It reduced the pension age to sixty-five years, provided a pension of 10/- a week for widows, 5/- for the first child, 3/- for any other child. Labour protested against the limited scope of this Act and to the contributory system. This Act created a widespread sense of grievance and injustice by excluding from its benefits thousands of women on the borderline of the rigid conditions laid down. For instance, the difference of a few weeks in the death of a husband, or lack of a few insurance contributions meant the loss of a pension. Many a sad story we had to listen to at our meetings, from widows who were victims of this injustice.

In the 1929 General Election, the Labour Party in its Manifesto, declared that the grave injustices of the existing Pension Acts would be immediately remedied. In March, the second Labour Government (again a minority one) came into office. In October, the first part of the Election pledge was fulfilled. Mr. Arthur Greenwood, who was Minister of Health, introduced an amending measure which came into force on January 1st, 1930. Over 500,000 women and children benefited immediately. The second part of the pledge was more difficult to carry out for a financial crisis swept the country. This was exploited politically and Labour was replaced by the so-called 'National' Government.

In 1937 when the Labour Party brought out a new Pension plan, there were nearly 300,000 Old Age Pensioners receiving Poor Law Relief because the pension was inadequate. Labour kept pressing for justice for the aged, but the war in 1939 gave the government an excuse to shelve the question.

Alongside the campaign for Old Age Pensions, the campaign for Mothers' Pensions was carried on by the women. The demand for Mothers' Pensions in this country was made as far back as 1908 at the Annual Conference of the Women's Labour League. The Annual Conferences of the Labour Party 1911-1912-1918-1921 and 1922 passed resolutions on Mothers' Pensions. The Trades Union Congress passed similar resolutions every year from 1916 to 1922. Mothers' Pensions were included in Labour's Election Manifesto in 1918 and 1922.

In 1919 and 1920 the subject was raised in Parliament, on behalf of the Labour Party by Mr. Tyson Wilson, M.P., who introduced a Bill to provide pensions for women and children covering the claim for Mothers' Pensions, but this had to be withdrawn.

In 1921 the Labour Party again presented its Mothers'

Pensions Bill which received a second reading but could not be carried further. Two years later Mr. R. J. Davies, M.P., moved a motion in the House on behalf of the Labour Party which differed very little from the Bill of 1920. A division was taken: 184 voted for and 248 against.

In 1919 the agitation for Mothers' Pensions received a great impetus from a visit paid to this country by Judge Henry Neil of Chicago, the father of Mothers' Pensions in America. He addressed meetings in many parts of this country, explaining what the United States had done for the widows and orphans.

When I was appointed Labour Women's Organiser, I received a letter from Mr. F.C. Potter of Cardiff, who had published some pamphlets on the American scheme, making an appeal to me to do all I could to get the women of Wales interested. He mentioned that Judge Henry Neil was on a visit to London and would like to visit South Wales. I got the Sections and Guilds in the Rhondda to organise public meetings for him.

I was privileged to entertain the Judge at my home. He told me he was going to devote all his time to touring and lecturing on Mothers' Pensions so that it became a 'universal act of justice' to the widows and orphans. Widows had no alternative in those days but Poor Law relief or the Workhouse. There was a severe means test if the widow gained a few shillings by taking in washing. If she had a piece of furniture that she could sell, her allowance was reduced. Many men, women and children of these brave mothers remember those days of great sacrifice.

Then there was the campaign for children's allowances which we called 'The Endowment of Motherhood'. It took Labour women some time to get the Party to accept this as policy. Trade Unionists feared that it would affect wages and wage negotiations. But it was accepted in the end and the country today enjoys the result of these strenuous efforts of our pioneers.

In 1945, when we had the First Labour Government

with a majority, the abolition of the Poor Law changed the whole structure of our Social Services. Poverty received its deathblow. It is up to this generation to see that it will never raise its ugly head again.

We are very proud in Wales that two of our Members of Parliament, Mr. James Griffiths (Llanelly) and Mr. Aneurin Bevan (Ebbw Vale) were destined to play such an important part in laying the foundations of the Welfare State which had brought about such great changes in the life of our people.

The Welfare State is in its infancy and is far from perfect. But it is only by trial and error that we learn. We who have lived through this silent revolutionary change are too near it to see its importance in the march of progress. But we must guard against indifference or abuse of the privileges that have been won for us.

Chapter Eleven
Any Other Business?

SINCE MY retirement I have had the opportunity of serving our people in other spheres — and I am very grateful for it. To have had to drop all public activities after a very busy life would have been very unfortunate for me.

In 1947 I was appointed by the Minster of Health — then Mr. Aneurin Bevan — to the Health Executive Council for Glamorgan. This opened a new field of interest and gave me a chance to play a part in bringing to fruition the reforms which the Labour Party had advocated for so long.

This appointment led me to membership of the Pontypridd and Rhondda Hospital Management Committee and I have been intensely interested in this work, particularly in the nursing side which is a special problem.

One of my main conclusions is that we must try and fill the gap between school-leaving at fifteen and the entry age for nursing training which is eighteen. At present we are loosing a large number of potential nurses because of this gap. We need a closer relationship between the hospital service and the education authorities on this matter. In this way we could prevent a lot of wastage and ensure that the best girls are presented for training.

The foundation of a good hospital service is an efficient and contented domestic and kitchen staff. This side of hospital work has had very little consideration up to now. The domestic staff must be given a proper status: it is impossible to try and run a hospital on the basis of casual labour. I am glad to see that the National Institute of Houseworkers has a scheme for training hospital domestic staff at its Centre in Swansea.

The other aspect of public work which has occupied me since my retirement has been my magistracy. I have served for thirty-two years as a Magistrate in the Ystrad Court, Rhondda.

There have been many changes since I first went on to the Bench. In 1924, when I was appointed, the Courts were still called 'Police Courts' and voluntary workers from religious and temperance organisations carried on the welfare work through a Police Court Mission. Now the name had been changed to Magistrates' Courts and a probation system with full-time officers has been established which is doing splendid work with young offenders. They also play an important part in the work of the Matrimonial Courts. Being a Magistrate brings great responsibility. Many seem to look upon this appointment more as a personal honour than as an opportunity for service to those who have fallen by the wayside.

In the Courts you are faced with the most intimate human relationships and some of the most tragic human problems. Dealing with young offenders needs a great deal of patience, an open mind, knowledge of social problems as they affect young people, a judicial mind to sift the evidence and, last but not least, plenty of common sense.

We are told that it is the offender and not the offence which should be our chief concern because we are dealing with a citizen in the making and we can make or mar his or her whole life by our decision. The best of our magistrates, who are prepared to specialise in the work and have an open mind to new ideas, should serve on the Juvenile Court panel.

Matrimonial cases are dealt with in a private court. The breaking up of married life and homes is a very sad affair, especially where there are children. From my experience, I should say that the chief pitfalls are the physical relation in marriage and financial arrangements in the home-making. For a young wife to be treated as a housekeeper and not a partner in financial matters in the home is asking for trouble. I advise would-be brides to get this little matter sorted before their wedding day!

Looking back on my life, one of the things that strikes me most strongly is the changes that have been brought about in homemaking, furnishing and fashions by the emancipation of women.

At the end of the last century and the beginning of this, married women always dressed in dark colours. To turn out in light and coloured clothes was a sign certainly of gaiety and often of something worse. The mother in a home was expected to make all the sacrifices. If she had a new dress or suit it had to last for many years. Often it was only when a death occurred in the family and mourning was bought with the insurance money that a mother had a new tailored suit.

I wonder how many young women today would like to go back to the fashions of those days? They would have to wear long trailing skirts with tight waists, high tight collars, well-boned bodices, flannel petticoats and chemises, and night dresses made of calico. Hats were enormous, covered in trimmings: an old photograph will tell women today what their grandmothers had to put up with. Today I find it hard sometimes to tell the difference between a mother and her daughter. I think that this is a wonderful change. Women are much healthier and happier because of it.

In the home the changes are even more incredible. Gone are all the old ugly wallpapers that made the rooms dark and dingy; gone are the large chests of draws, the big dining table, the overmantle gathering dust and the what-not full of bits and pieces of china. There are no more long lace curtains draped over the windows, and the aspidistra or geranium plant in a pot has vanished with them.

In those days stone floors had to be scoured with sand and ugly grates took an hour or so to polish with blacklead — and lots of coal to start a fire as well.

The home is a woman's workshop, but more than that, it can

reflect her personality. In it she can create the environment which will make her family feel that 'there is no place like home' and an impression that will last all through their lives.

Do not be afraid of colour! All women should understand its effect on everyday life. It can have a real effect on our health and our tempers. Rooms need to be restful but cheerful. They cannot be cheerful without colour, and they are not restful if there is a clash of colours. There is so much that can be done in this field of today when tradition and superstition in decoration are things of the past.

I had to try and teach women not to be afraid of freedom. I think today that we must encourage them not to fear the future. I hope that what I have written of the changes that have taken place in the last fifty years will help younger women.

They can draw their own conclusions on their debt to the great Labour movement with its three paths to power for the people: as the citizens move through the Labour Party; as workers through the Trade Unions; and the consumers through the Co-operative Movement.

All progressive movements go through the same phases. At first they are ignored; then when their power grows their leaders are persecuted; finally they are recognised. No reactionary Government can ignore the Labour Movement, but it can hinder its forward march: but then only if the workers themselves give it political power by their votes!

I end with the words of William Morris, the great Socialist poet and visionary:

> *'Then come let us cast off fooling*
> *And put by ease and rest*
> *For the Cause alone is worthy*
> *Till the good days bring the best!'*

APPRECIATION

My grateful thanks to George Viner of the Daily Herald,
Chairman of Cymric Democrat Publishing Society,
for his assistance in the preparation of this book.

POLITICAL WRITINGS

1923 — 1948

January 1923

THE COLLIERY WORKER'S MAGAZINE
THE WOMEN'S PAGE

A Message to Wives and Mothers of All Men who work in and around the Mines of South Wales and Monmouthshire

This Magazine is launching out on its first Mission on the first month of the New Year, 1923. May it take its message of Hope and Good Wishes that this coming year will be brighter and better for all the Workers of this country.

The Mission of this Magazine is chiefly to convey the Truth to all Workers concerning their own Industry, and through its columns we hope to get in touch with the Wives and Mothers of all Colliery Workers, and to discuss from time to time matters that affect the women, both Industrially and Politically.

We look around and travel from place to place, what do we find? The same appalling conditions everywhere, through low wages and unemployment. Men and women that have been thrifty all their lives come to the end of their life-long savings long ago, and having to seek Parish Relief.

Men and women who have struggled to own their own houses, by sacrifice and hard struggle, having to mortgage them to get food.

Fathers and Mothers who have saved to give their children a chance of a good education, having to spend all, and no hope of carrying out their hearts' desire to give their children a good start in life.

With the low wages today, no mother can do justice to her family; 30/- to 45/- a week with a family from one to six or eight children to feed and clothe, is humanly impossible.

The cost of living now stands at about 80 per cent above the

1914 standard. Then there is the rent to be considered, which is taking away every week from 7/- to 15/-. But the Property Owners are not satisfied: they are asking the Government Rent Act Inquiry Committee to recommend another increase of 20 per cent on House Rent, their plea being that they cannot make both ends meet.

Is it any wonder that the women, who are the Chancellors of the Exchequer of the home, lose their heart under such a struggle? It's enough to make the stoutest heart break. If there ever were any heroines, they are to be found in the homes of the Mineworker today. This condition of things should make all the women think, and ask the question, What is wrong? There must be a cause for all this. Yes, my friends, there is a cause, and we hope, through the medium of this Magazine, to deal with the Cause, and also to suggest the Remedy.

Mr. Stephen Walsh, one of the Miners' MPs, in opening up the debate on the Miners' Right to Live, in the House of Commons on December 14th 1922, pointed out that no industry has suffered more unemployment than the Coal Mining Industry. The reductions in wages amounted to about £3,000,000 a week.

What does this mean to the women? £3,000,000 a week less purchasing power, which means less food, less clothes, less household goods, a lower standard of living.

Less food means a lowering of the physique, and a low physique means less resistance to combat disease germs. The best resistance to disease is to get a healthy body, but to get a healthy body we must have good food, good clothing and a good home. To get these we must have good wages, which is the basis of our purchasing power for a good standard of life. Therefore, Industrial matters and Politics are of vital importance to all women. If mothers are to do the noble job of 'fitting the child for the world', she will also have to 'fit the world for the child'. To fit the child for the world, the child must have a healthy body, and to get this he must have good food, good clothing, and a good home.

To make the world fit for the child, it must be made free from Wars, Unemployment, Disease, Bad Housing, and Poverty; and to do that, the mothers must take a keener interest in these matters.

Then there is the question of Pit Baths to reduce the laborious work of women in the home. This question will be dealt with in a further issue of this Magazine.

We want better Compensation Laws in connection with the Mining Industry. More safeguards to preserve life and limb. The application of more modern machinery in and at the Pits to reduce the laborious work of the Miner.

Anyone who visited the Engineers Exhibition which was held at Cardiff last November could not but be impressed with the inventions displayed there on these lines, and make one ask the question, Why could not these inventions be applied to Industry, so as to benefit mankind?

All these great changes are long overdue, and they will come about when the workers Will them.

In conclusion, I want to make an appeal to all the Mineworkers to get the womenfolk to read this Magazine, and, if possible, to contribute to it by way of questions, letters, or short articles on all matters that affect the lives of Mineworkers.

May this Magazine realise its Mission, and meet with every success, 'for Knowledge is Power'.

THE COLLIERY WORKER'S MAGAZINE
THE WOMEN'S PAGE

Pit-head Baths

The Need for Renewed Agitation and Legislation

All readers interested in this question must feel pleased with the resolution passed at the Annual Conference of the South Wales Miners' Federation held in June last, on this important question.

But we must all realise that there is something more to be done than passing resolutions before Pithead Baths become a reality in the South Wales Coalfield, and that something more is an Extensive Agitation on the matter, followed by the wholehearted support of all the Colliery Workers, having the full knowledge of what this change of custom will mean to themselves, their wives and families, and using their industrial and political power with every determination that Pithead Baths shall become a reality in their own lifetime.

Last, but not least, we shall need the co-operation and wholehearted support of the womenfolk of all the mining areas, who will stand shoulder to shoulder with the men in the fight for these facilities, which will help to humanise the Mining Industry.

At the present time, this question is a controversial one among the miners themselves, and my experience teaches me that there is a great need for education on the matter, hence the suggestion of our Extensive Agitation.

Ignorance blocks the way of progress on this question like

all other reforms, and some of the objections raised at various meetings have not come along the path of knowledge on the matter, or else they would never have been asked.

There is also another factor to combat on this question of Pitbaths, namely, that we in Wales are such slaves to custom, that because our grandfathers and our fathers came home black, that it must continue so.

But the fathers of today must throw off this old idea of custom, and remember that 'new times demands new methods,' and that we must adapt ourselves to these new occasions, realising that by doing so in this matter, we shall be making the lot of the next generation much brighter and the task of the womenfolk in the mining areas much easier.

As things are at present, it is not only the men that are employed by the Mineowners, but their wives are also employed (without pay) to clear up the dirt in the homes that ought to have been left at the pit top.

But some friends will say, 'Give us baths in the home, then we will not want Pit baths'. I quite agree we need a bath in every home, but we shall also need the Pit baths. Baths in the home will mean still bringing home the dirt from the Pit, still the work of drying the Pit clothes in the home. Pithead baths would take all that away.

I would like to quote a few more objections raised by some of the workers themselves, which are as follows:

'That the men will have to rise earlier in the morning, and dress twice'. 'That they will catch cold by using the baths'. 'Who would wash the men's backs?', and in some cases, men are afraid to get their backs washed more often than once a week because their grandfather believed it would weaken their spine. 'Who is going to dry the clothes?'. 'How were the clothes going to be mended?'. That the men would have to change when they had a load of coal to carry in.

Unfortunately it is the custom in some homes for the women to carry the coal in to save the men when they get home tired.

It is high time this custom was done away with. I have come across many sad cases of suffering among women as a result of doing this job.

What is the changing of a suit of clothes compared with the suffering of the mothers and wives which this job entails?

These are but a few of the questions, but let us compare them with the larger issues involved in this question. What would Pit baths really mean? It would mean shorter hours, less drudgery, dirty work for the women. More rest. More leisure.

Less physical strain on the mothers. No need for handling and lifting of heavy tubs and boilers. Healthier mothers, brighter mothers, cleaner and brighter homes. Higher standard of cleanliness – individually, in the home, and in the community. Raise the status of the Miner in Society.

Pithead baths and properly-equipped Ambulance rooms, and other facilities, would help to humanise the Mining Industry very considerably.

Before the last lock-out, the Labour women carried on a campaign, urging all the Lodges to form Pithead Baths Provisional Committees, and a number of suggestions were drafted as a basis of work and discussion for the committees, which were as follows:

SUGGESTIONS

1. To arouse interest and to carry on propaganda on Pitbaths in the Districts.

2. To prepare suggestions of schemes to put before the Mineowners as to what kinds of Pit baths and other facilities are needed by the miners.

3. To prepare a Constitution for Pit Baths Committees to submit to Mineowners re. function, representation of miners and their wives.

QUESTIONS FOR DISCUSSION

1. Building – Whether dressing-room with baths in separate

corridors, or dressing-room and baths in same room.

2.Cubicles – whether of glazed tiles or corrugated iron. Whether compartment or two compartments (inner with spray bath and outer for dressing and fitted with seat and peg).

3.Need for separate room or locker for clean clothes.

4.Provision for drying pit clothes.

5.Provision for mending pit clothes.

6.Provision for washing pit clothes.

7.Provision for soap and towels.

8.Canteen at pit tops for hot drinks.

9.Sanitary arrangements.

10.Properly equipped Ambulance Room attached to pit baths.

What we need today is put in the following lines of William Morris:

> *'Intelligence enough to Conceive*
> *Courage enough to Will*
> *Power enough to Compel.'*

So let our slogan on this question be:

'Agitate, Educate and Organise'

I would heartily invite readers to open up correspondence, expressing their views on this question of Pit baths, and to forward same before the 20th of next month to the following address: Mrs. E. Andrews, Ruskin House, 73, Bailey Street, Ton Pentre.

July 1924

THE COLLIERY WORKER'S MAGAZINE
THE WOMEN'S PAGE

Housing — The Women's Problem

The women all over the country will no doubt welcome Mr Wheatley's Housing Bill. It is the most courageous Housing Bill that has ever been placed before Parliament, and we are hoping that it is going to pass through all the stages in the House of Commons until it becomes law, and then we can proceed with Housing without any further delay.

Two other Bills have been before the House these last few years.

Dr. Addison made the first attempt, and his Bill gave us 200,000, but Dr. Addison was too progressive for his Government, and thus he resigned, and Sir Alfred Mond took his place. The man of 'One room for married people' fame.

Sir Alfred cried a halt to this Housing Scheme. We then had a General Election and Mr. Neville Chamberlain brought in a second scheme of 53,000, but the majority of the houses are built for sale and not to let. Thus this scheme does not meet the crying need of the workers who cannot afford to buy, but have to rent.

Mr Wheatley in his Bill wants to solve the Housing of the Industrial and Agricultural Workers of the country first.

Attempts are made by many of the politicians of the other parties to discourage this Bill. Mr. Lloyd George stated at a meeting the other day that 'This Bill is the formation of a big Trust in Housing.'

It is nothing of the kind. This Bill simply means the co-operation of the Government, the master builder, manufacturers and Operatives, to try and solve this Housing Problem for the sake of humanity, and anyone who travels from place to place will realise the appalling misery and degradation that prevails because of bad housing. Anyone who attends the Courts of our country will find that lack of Housing and bad housing is more responsible for quarrels and separation orders than any other factor at present.

Two or three apartments in one house, lack of accommodation, make people irritable with each other, which finally ends in blows and Court proceedings.

This Bill is going to pay special attention to the Housing problem in Rural Areas. The Housing problem is serious in the Industrial Areas, but visiting the country districts will prove that as far as ventilation and sanitation are concerned, it is more serious in the Rural Areas.

I have recently visited Montgomeryshire and spent a few hours visiting the slums of Welshpool. For a small town with ideal surroundings, one would hardly expect to find such slumdom.

Behind the main street there were rows of Houses called Passages. These were the conditions: No back doors, one water tap outside for every four or five houses, one w.c. for every two houses, open gutters. At the top of one passage was a slaughter-house. Most of the houses were one room up and one down. Some had little slopes. The narrow path between the houses were either pebbled or covered with large, rough stones. The refuse was tipped in little heaps, where the ash cart called twice a week to clear away.

The houses were occupied chiefly by agricultural workers, who earned about 15/- a week. They and their little families had to be herded under these conditions, while all around were beautiful land and scenery.

While going through these Passages, a little poem came to my mind which was really typical of the position as far as the children were concerned.

> *Dozens of children playing*
> *In a narrow dirty street,*
> *Smooth clean roads for motors*
> *Stones for the babies' feet.*
>
> *Fields set apart for pheasants,*
> *Room for the farmer's hay,*
> *Yet no where 'mid all the green acres*
> *A room where a child could play.*
>
> *No room in the houses for children,*
> *And little room outside;*
> *Would there be room in Heaven*
> *I wonder 'If they died.'*

It is no good people lecturing to the women living under these conditions just described about cleanliness and the danger of flies in the Summer time.

No woman can hope to combat dirt and disease under these conditions. Give the women decent homes, proper sanitation, and decent standard of living, then there will be less need of lectures on subjects as mentioned above.

Mr Wheatley's Bill suggests a Housing Programme extending over 15 years on the following basis:

1925...... 90,000
1926......100,000
1927......110,000
1928......120,000
1929......135,000
1930......150,000
1931......170,000
1932......190,000

1933......210,000
1934......225,000

This will approximately mean that in 15 years we shall have about two and a half million new houses built.

It will also mean that by that time we shall have twelve and a half million of our people living under decent conditions.

This is a memorial that would be worthy of the first Labour Government in this country.

It depends upon the women of this country whether this Bill becomes an established fact. Unseen forces are getting to work against this Bill, but we as women can counteract it by creating that public opinion in the country which is the greatest factor towards getting any reforms.

The Home is the Woman's Workshop. It is the most important workshop in the land, so it is up to us to see to it that the Homes of the Workers will get the legislation and attention they deserve.

The women must also see to it that they get working women on all the Housing Committees in connection with the Local Authorities; also that Women's Sections and Co-operative Guilds should set up Special Committees so that they could submit suggestions to the Housing Committee with all the Labour saving devices possible to make the lot of our Working Women easier for the future.

Now is the time to move in the matter. It will be too late when the houses are built.

I trust that the women who will read this article will get busy in their districts in this respect, and thus carry on a great Crusade on Housing all through the country.

October 1924

THE COLLIERY WORKERS' MAGAZINE
THE WOMEN'S PAGE

Women and World Peace

'Mothers, in your hands, more than in those of any others,
lies the salvation of the world.' Tolstoy

Important events have taken place these last few weeks in connection with international problems and towards world peace that I feel I must write this month on these lines.

All who think and read must feel overjoyed at the work accomplished by our worthy Prime Minister, Mr James Ramsay Macdonald. With his honesty and sincerity of purpose, he has been the means of creating a new spirit of hope and goodwill among the nations of the world, which is the foundation on which we can build towards establishing World Peace.

The acceptance of the Dawes Report is the first step. We might not quite agree with all it implies, but the fact still remains that it is a great accomplishment to get all the representative nations around a table together, and to come to one common agreement.

Mr. Lloyd George held 13 Conferences and failed. Mr Ramsay Macdonald held one Conference and succeeded, simply because he has adopted the attitude of 'Come brothers, let us reason together.'

The League of Nations Conference, at the time of writing promises to be a success, whereby its machinery will become a important factor to settle International disputes.

There are still some people who believe that war is inevitable, that they come and go according to divine plan. They have no faith in human nature. Many prominent politicians have spoken a great deal about human nature and its failings, but, friends, when we reflect we find that human nature, with its finer instincts, has done great deeds of heroism and sacrifice.

We find these finer qualities expressed in our home life, in our industries, men prepared to lay down their lives for their comrades when in danger, women prepared to lay down their lives for their children. These deeds are done by human beings. What we want to do is to cultivate these finer instincts and change of state of society, which is the cause very largely of developing the lower instincts at the expense of the finer instincts. The teaching of false patriotism, racial hatred which leads to war, exploiting the instinct of fear, bad environment, bad housing, low wages — these are the seeds which develop the base in human nature. War is the basest of all crimes. War causes the greatest magnitude of suffering, but it also involves and justifies all other crimes.

What Women can do.

Women have a great part to play in establishing World Peace. If we want to become a peace-loving nation, the mother of today has to start to train the mind of her child in the ideals of Peace. That is the first step. H.N. Brailsford once stated that 'Armies may destroy armies, but no army ever destroyed Militarism, because it is a state of mind'.

In the past, it has been easier to get men to fight than to think. It is the work of women, mothers and teachers, to create the right impression to the mind of the child. The first step is to see that the children of today get no Toy Guns, Toy Pistols, Toy Swords, no dressing them up in soldier clothes, no picture books about War and all its glories — we know what War is and all its horrors. What have these toy implements to do with War? some of my readers may ask. Very much, my friends. These toy implements, although to our minds they appear very innocent, they have a psychological effect upon the plastic mind of the child. Have you ever watched children playing in the street with these toys? They always play killing each other. Why, they are the toys of destruction, and when these are given to the children they create the idea that playing as soldiers means that they must get an enemy, and an enemy to kill. We can also go further, and get men and women on our Local Authorities who will see to it that the children get no Military Drills, no War picture books and history, and no teaching of False Patriotism.

We should also see that the Picture of War should not be exhibited in our Cinemas. The Local Authorities can use their power to censor these pictures, and thus, by the co-operation of mothers, teachers, councillors and Churches, we can help to create a new mind towards Peace and Brotherhood. Benjamin Kidd in his book, 'Science of Power', has proved his theory:'Give me the young, and I will create a new mind and a new world in a single generation.'

May I appeal to all my women readers to help in this great work. The call comes to us today, especially as women, by helping to create the new mind and making the world free from War. We shall save the lives of the boys of today when they become the men of the future, we shall prevent broken hearts of mothers, fathers, wives and sisters. We shall prevent the breaking of human lives and the shattering of human flesh, and thus hand down to the next generation a foundation whereby the can build on, where reason shall reign supreme in the settling of disputes between nations.

The following illustration will give us an example of what has been done between two States to settle a dispute, and which is possible between two nations:

'On March 13th, 1904, there was created on a pinnacle of the Andes Mountains, 13,000 feet above the sea, and on the very boundary line fixed between Argentina and Chili a statue of Christ holding the Cross. It is 26 feet high, and stands on a pedestal of granite, symbolising the world. The statue itself was cast out of cannon balls. The inscription at its base, in granite, says 'These mountains will crumble to dust ere Argentines and Chileans will break the Peace which at the feet of Christ the Redeemer they have sworn to keep.' The exact position of this boundary had been a cause of dispute for over half-a-century; indeed, the feuds to which it gave rise existed as long ago as 1833, and twice the nations had been on the verge of war. At last, both parties were persuaded to submit their quarrel to arbitration, and our Queen Victoria was chosen as the arbitrator. She died before the matter was settled, and so King Edward gave the award. The satisfaction and joy this gave seems to have suggested the idea of the statue of Christ, which was to be a witness in future times of the relations of peace and goodwill between the people.'

I would welcome the views of the women readers on this subject.

March 1925

THE COLLIERY WORKERS' MAGAZINE
THE WOMEN'S PAGE

Women's Work in Local Elections.

Before this Magazine gets into the hands of our readers, the results of the County Council Elections will be made known to us.

It is difficult to forecast the results at the time of writing, but they will be some criterion of the results of the Urban Council and Guardian Elections which will take place next month.

I doubt very much whether we realise the importance of Local Government and its possibilities to make the life of the Community brighter, healthier, and happier.

During the contest, we shall, no doubt hear very much about the Rates, and our opponents will promise us better Education, better Housing and better everything, and keep down the Rates. They cannot do both, so let us not be deceived with the **'Down with the Rates Stunt.'** What Labour wants is the full value for the **rates we pay**.

The question of Local Government is a very big one, and it would be impossible for me to deal with it in all its phases in one article, so I want to confine myself to a few matters of vital interest to the women, and to reforms that are on the Statute Book, but are permissive clauses in the Acts of Parliament, which simply means that the Council **May** do this or that, but needs public opinion to turn the **May** into **Must**.

The following are matters of interest, and should be raised in the coming Elections: (1) A Clean Milk Supply. (2) Home Help Scheme in connection with Maternity Work. (3) Open-

Air Nursery Schools for children aged two to six years of age.

Clean Milk

The dirty milk supply we get in this country is responsible more than any other article of Food for Disease and the spread of Tuberculosis. There is abundant proof that Cholera, Typhoid, Scarlet Fever, Diphtheria, epidemic Diarrhoea and Tuberculosis are all frequently caused by Milk.

Professor J.P Buxton speaking at a Farmers' Club, London, in December last, stated it was estimated that 30 per cent of the cattle of this country were affected by Tuberculosis, and approximately 30 per cent had tubercular udders.

Mr. Henry Gray, a well known veterinary Surgeon, also stated that 30 per cent, and in many cases 50 per cent, of the dairy cattle in this country are affected with Tuberculosis and that cattle owners possessing pedigree herds, when they find a cow infected with tuberculosis, sell them to Dairy farmers. He also points out that no intelligent breeder of pedigree cattle would allow a calf to suckle or to get into contact with an infected cow. Yet, **the Milk that is not good enough for a pedigree calf, is good enough for the Nation's children**. Is it any wonder that this disease is so rampant? 30,000 to 40,000 people died in 1923 from Tuberculosis, and our Sanatoriums are full. What is the use of spending the nation's money on trying to cure disease, when a **Clean Milk Supply would prevent it?**

Sir George Newman in one of his reports states that people must be taught that **Tuberculosis** is not necessarily **hereditary**, and therefore **predestined**, but is the result of personal infection or drinking Tuberculosis **Milk**.

We, as woman, must therefore agitate in this Election for a Municipal Milk Supply Depot, where the milk could be Pasteurized, and thus guarantee the Community a Clean Milk Supply.

Haverfordwest, Pembrokeshire, has led the way in Wales, like Bradford led the way in England. This question is urgent and it is vital.

Home Helps

We must also agitate for service of Home Helps as part of Maternity Work of the Councils where the mothers could get some reliable persons to come in and look after her during confinement.

At present, a large percentage of the mothers have to depend on neighbours, or a little schoolgirl, or the husband has to remain home from work, and she has to do many jobs in bed for her little ones, sitting up the second and third day and getting up very often too soon because the Home duties are so pressing. Home Helps would meet with the needs of mothers as well as open up a **New Avenue** of Employment for our Girls.

The following figures will prove this point. There are approximately 5,000 births in the Rhondda in the year. If only 5 per cent of the mothers had the service of Home Helps for one week only, we would need at present one hundred Home Helps. 5 per cent is a very low figure to estimate, but it will suffice to prove the possibilities of this New Avenue of Employment for our Girls.

Open-Air Nursery Schools

The establishment of Open-Air Nursery Schools for children from two years would be a boon for little ones as well as Mothers. Miss Margaret McMillan has pioneered this reform, and her experiment at Deptford has proved that they can cure the little ones from Rickets, Anaemia and prevents Adenoids simply by open air, light and sunshine. Sir George Newman states that nine out of every ten children born are healthy, and before they reach the age of two years about 50 per cent of them are damaged in health. Thus the Open-Air Nursery School would help to make these little ones healthy and bonnie. What a boon these Schools would be for Mothers who have two or three little ones under five years of age, where the little ones could be cared for and nurtured, and be out of danger from the street traffic.

Space will not permit me to write fuller details this time. I shall deal with these details in future articles, but I want to point out that these matters are permissive clauses. Let us therefore see to it with all earnestness we possess, and press our future Councillors for the promise that they will help to turn those **Mays** into **Musts** for the sake of the women and little children.

> *'Inasmuch as ye have done it unto these little ones,*
> *ye have done it unto Me.'*

January 1926

THE COLLIERY WORKERS' MAGAZINE
THE WOMEN'S PAGE

A Happy New Year

'Our young men are seeing visions,
Our old men are dreaming dreams,
And on mountain peaks already
Rising sun of wisdom gleams.'

Francis G. Hanchett

A Happy New Year to all. We have left 1925 behind us and are facing1926 with a clouded and troubled horizon. With problems that overwhelm us, we would despair but for **Faith and Vision**.

Labour hopes for the future, and urges us on to greater efforts and determination this year to try and remove the cause of all this misery and destitution.

In the mining industry we are almost hoping for some miracle to be performed in May. I hear many miners' wives say **we cannot hope much until May, then things may become better**, and the gleam of hope in their eyes when they say it shows that they mean it. One marvels at the hope and patience of those who suffer so much. It is this **Hope** that keeps them from despair.

'The present system is based on the patience of the poor,' is one of Dan Griffiths' sayings. How true this statement in the light of present-day affairs.

At a meeting the other day it was reported that there were little children in Blaina district, three years of age, who have never walked, and very little hopes of walking under the present conditions.

The children are suffering from rickets — a disease of **illnourishment and darkness**, which simply means lack of proper nourishing foods, fresh air and sunshine.

Unemployment, with its attendants, **disease and death**, have stalked through this district these last few years, and its effects will be felt by the next generation.

What is the remedy? The Prime Minister says, Less Wages, Work harder, Longer Hours.

What does his Government promise us? More Taxes on Cutlery, Gas Mantles. Laces and Embroidery, Fabric Gloves, Packing and Wrapping Paper, under the guise of Safeguarding of Industries Bill; Unemployment — young men being scrapped off the Live Registers because their parents are working.

Economy in Education

Circular 1371, issued recently by the Board of Education, suggesting a Block Grant System, has aroused all thinking people and progressive Local Authorities. It is the most reactionary document ever issued from the Board of Education. It has even shocked some of the Lords in the Second Chamber.

What does it mean? Instead of 50 per cent of expenses on Education to be borne out of National Taxation a block grant will be given to each Authority with a **do as you like sort of business.** If your Education costs more, the Local Authority will have to go, cap in hand, to the Board of Education to ask for more, like Oliver Twist. A refusal will mean an increase in the rates.

All children under five years of age are not to be admitted to schools, and 30 per cent taken off the grant per child under five, which will mean economy on the **Nursery Schools**. There are at present 211,003 children under five years attending school.

Lord Somers, replying in the House of Lords on behalf of the Government on December 15th, stated: **'In the opinion of the Government, generally speaking, a child under five years of age should be at home and not at School.'**

Lord Eustace Percy, Minister of Education, replying on behalf of the Government, on Thursday December 17th, stated: **'As to children under five, his view was that sending them to school was a local habit rather than a social necessity.'**

How little these people know of the lot of the workers!

The wives of Lords, Industrial Magnates and Shareholders can engage nurses for their children; have day and night nurseries, plenty of open spaces inside and outside their homes. But what about the little ones who live in crowded homes, where the overworked mother is expected to be nurse, cook, washerwoman, dressmaker, etc., etc.?

Mr, Trevelyan, Labour ex-Minister of Education, reminded the House in his speech on December 17th, **that there were hundreds and thousands of children who haunted the mean streets of our cities whose fate it was to sit on the kerbstones with feet in the gutter, whose mothers were out all day working; and how much better it would be for them to be in clean, dry, well-ventilated schoolrooms.** A blessing to both mother and children.

The Tory Government have given this notorious Circular their blessing in the House of Commons on December 17th. But owing to the pressure of public opinion against this Circular, Lord Eustace Percy, the Minister of Education, may have to postpone its operation for one year, and by the end of the year **for good**, we hope.

Sir Joynson-Hicks, speaking the other day, said 'We cannot afford to live as we are.' Our Education is costing us 40 million pounds out of the National Purse — £1 per head of the population. But we can waste £12 per head of the population on War. Plenty of money and no grumbling for destroying life and blowing out brains but waste to spend money on Educating Brains. That is the outlook of our glorious Government. The whole cost of Education last year from National and Local taxation amounted to £69,860,000 but we can afford to pay £350 million a year of interest to people on War Loans, and £115 million a year to the Army, Navy and Air force.

How long will the workers allow this to go on? When I hear audiences singing, 'When wilt thou save the people,' I feel we can ask, When will the people save themselves?

Let us this New Year go forward, renewing our faith in the Cause, renewing our faith in each other, equipping ourselves with knowledge and co-operating together to remove all the obstacles that hinder us in our progress towards a more, just and humane Society.

> *'Then, come let us cast off fooling,*
> *And put by ease and rest;*
> *For the cause alone is worthy,*
> *Till the good days bring the best'*

William Morris

April 1926

THE COLLIERY WORKER'S MAGAZINE
THE WOMEN'S PAGE

The Women's Part in the National Crisis

We are facing an unprecedented crisis these days in the Mining Industry. A crisis which not only affects the Miners and their families, but all other workers in the country as well.

Therefore, it behoves us all, both men and women, to put our 'thinking caps' on and get all the knowledge we can, so as to achieve greater unity and solidarity among all workers than has ever been experienced before in any Industrial Crisis.

The most powerful weapons the miners can have in this struggle will be a **100 per cent Trade Unionism, 100 per cent support and co-operation of their womenfolk, and 100 per cent confidence in our Leaders.**

Disunity, disloyalty; suspicion, distrust, will destroy and weaken our fight, **but unity, loyalty and faith in our cause and each other, will help us to win.**

Dividing the Women

Great effort is being made to organise the women, especially the miners' wives, into the 'Women's Guild of Empire,' led by General Flora Gummond. She calls it a 'Common Sense League,' and its chief object is to **'Stop Strikes and Lock-outs.'** She has been busy in the South Wales Coalfield lately organising the miners' wives for a Demonstration to be held in London on Saturday, April 17th. Cheap fares have been arranged, and the promise of a good outing. Unfortunately a number of miners' wives are linking themselves up with this Demonstration without realising that by doing so **they betray their men in their fight for a decent existence,** which will retaliate on themselves in due course. It is up to us to do all we can **to save these women from themselves.**

The outing is a temptation to many women, but times are far too serious to sacrifice our welfare for an Outing, and no woman who understands, and is concerned about the welfare of her husband and family, would be so foolish as to join in a Demonstration of this kind.

Coal Commission Report

By now, everybody will have some idea of the proposals put forward in the Coal Commission's Report. Proposals like Better Housing for the Miners, Pithead Baths, and Holidays with Pay, are proposals that we can all agree, and are the outcome of years of agitation by the Miners' Federation and Labour Party; but when it comes to **Wages,** which is the crux of the present crisis, then comes the parting of the ways.

Suggested Family Allowance

A scheme of Family Allowance has been suggested, and we need to be very guarded on this point. Family Allowance under **Socialism** would be the ideal thing, because the fundamental principle would be according to individual needs, and the right of the full development of each individual. For that development we need more than Food, Clothing and Shelter, we need, in addition, Books, Music, Flowers, Recreation, Travel and Leisure.

To adopt a family allowance under a Capitalist system with the present basis, which is nothing but a 'Fodder Basis,' will violate a great Socialistic principle for private gains.

If the Subsistence Allowance offered by the Mineowners

to the Miners last August is any criterion of the Commission and Mineowners' idea of Family Allowance, then, I say, it will not only violate a great principle, but is **an insult** to the intelligence of the Miners and their families.

It is well to reflect for a moment on these terms, viz., Standard Basis Rates: 5/. Allowances, wife, 1/3, equal 6/3, plus 5d. for first child, 4d. for second, 3d. for the third, 2d. for the fourth and nothing for the rest.

Highest rate, 6/10½, wife nothing, and the same rate for the children; 1/3 per day to meet the needs of four children.

Picture a family of four children sitting around a table; the mother will put in front of the eldest five penny buns, four for the second, three for the third, and two for the youngest. There you have the picture of the full allowance for one day, according to this basis. If the youngest happens to be a baby, it will cost at least 6/- or 7/- a week to feed on dried milk.

These are the terms offered in Subsistence Allowance of last August, which makes one realise the very low value the Mineowners put on the workers' children.

It is our job, nay, our duty, in this struggle to make employers and the Government realise that the needs of the Miners' children are the same exactly as the needs of their own children.

We must raise the standard of Human Values, and it is **We** alone who can do it.

Women! Rally round your men folk in this Great Fight. They will need your help and inspiration. **Men!** Encourage your Women; have patience, and spare a little time to explain this problem to them, so that, with understanding and co-operation, no one dare divide us by cheap outings, demonstrations, cups of tea, or false statements.

Let us, then, get our Wits sharpened and our Weapons ready for the fray.

100 per cent Trade Unionism.

100 per cent Support and Co-operation of the Womenfolk.
100 per cent Confidence in our Leaders.

And we shall win.

Mass Meetings for Miners' Wives will be held in the Coalfield. Please Rally, and bring your friends with you.

May 1926

THE COLLIERY WORKER'S MAGAZINE
THE WOMEN'S PAGE

Divide And Rule

At the time of writing this article, the destiny of the miners is in the 'Lap of the Gods' as far as any settlement is concerned, and it is difficult to say what may happen in the next few weeks.

To follow the leading articles of the Capitalist Press these days is indeed humorous, were things not so serious, and the livelihood of our people at stake.

One day you will have them very sympathetic towards the Unemployed Miner, and set him against the Employed Miner, next day it will be the Married men against the Unmarried. Another day they will divide the community: 'Miners versus the Public.' Then another day bouquets will be thrown at miners at the expense of their leaders. Another time they will appeal to prejudice, will exploit the instinct of Fear, will misrepresent the miners' case, and last, but not least, will appeal to your sympathy by placards on 'The Losses of Local Collieries' and articles giving an account of the hardships of the Mineowners.

What is the object of all this? **Divide and Rule.** Divide you into Districts, Divide you into Sections. Because it is only by doing this 'Capitalism can exist.'

The only way to Peace and Prosperity will be the Nationalisation of Mines, and run the industry because we need coal for use and not only to make Profits for individuals. If all the leaders and agitators in Movement stopped preaching

Nationalisation tomorrow **force of circumstances** will compel the nation, sooner or later, to take over the mines to save the country from bankruptcy. The present system in Industry has throttled itself; so it is our duty to prepare ourselves for this inevitable change, where the workers will have to share the responsibility and prosperity for the Common Good.

What about the Women?

The Press and the Guild of Empire have also been busy to divide the women for the same object. We have just had exaggerated news about this demonstration, as far as numbers are concerned. Women demonstrating against Strikes — and Lock-outs added as an afterthought! What a farce! Women on horseback leading! **'They must be the Miners' Wives, who, after sending their husbands to work, can spend their mornings riding in Rotten Row, Hyde Park,'** and following in their train were 'Workers' Wives,' who have been used as tools against their men folk in their struggle for **Right to Live.**

Then we read in the Press how some of the Workers' Wives made speeches in the Albert Hall, and one was a miner's wife from South Wales.

What a pity that we have so many Mrs. Henry Dubbs in the country. **Socialists** have been charged as **Home Breakers!** Who are the real home-breakers today but the people who will try and influence wives against their husbands just to maintain the present system?

We have not only got the Mrs. Henry Dubbs that will join the demonstrations just for a cheap outing, but we have many Mrs. Henry Dubbs that have been writing letters to the Press on how cheap they can live and rear a family.

One woman writes how she can keep a family of 15 people on 45/- a week. She must be super-human to accomplish this feat. Here are some of the items in her Budget: Rent, 7/-; meat,

2/-; cheese, 2d; tea, ¼ lb; no vegetables; two candles, 1d., etc. She must be sending some of the children out to graze to do this.

This is only another stunt to help keep down wages. When women will put more value on themselves and their children, they will be ashamed to boast of budgets of this kind to show how cheaply they can live, but will demand a fairer share of the good things that are produced, so as to build up healthy and virile men and women.

Some weeks ago there was an article in one of our Capitalist Daily Papers, with big headlines, 'The Best-Fed Fighter — Tommy's Menu' and it gave a list of Tommy's Menu for a week, and stated that the Chemists of the Army Medical Board had been studying Tommy's Diet to find out the food values. And for what? To prepare for War.

We have posters urging young men to join the Army, with a promise of Good Pay, Good Clothes, Good Housing, Education, Good Sport, Opportunities for Promotion, and Travel.

It is when the same facilities will be given to the Workers who produce so that **we might live,** it is then, and then only, can we have Peace in Industry. When we can boast of the **'Best-Fed Worker'**, the **happiest and most intelligent Worker,** it will be a far better credit to us as a civilised and Christian nation.

That is one of the aims of **Socialism.** That is the conflict underlying this struggle. Pre-War standard and lower wages will not bring it about. So let us carry on with this fight, and stand solid by our men, whatever the cost. Rally to all our meetings. Get knowledge on the problem which will give us strength and wisdom to do the right thing at the right time.

'Were half the power that fills the world with terror,
Were half the Wealth bestowed on Camps and Courts,
Given to redeem the Human Mind from error,

There were no need for arsenals or forts.'

Lowell

If you want the truth about the crisis read the **'Daily Herald'** — Labour's Own Paper.

August 1926

THE COLLIERY WORKER'S MAGAZINE
THE WOMEN'S PAGE

Something that a Tory Government Cannot Do

The present Tory Government, with its huge majority, can do many things to coerce the workers. It can repeal the Seven Hours Bill, it can vote for £3,000,000 in its estimates to purchase coal from abroad to beat the miners in their fight, it can, by the passing of one small Bill, take over the control of the Poor Law at West Ham, which will take the power from the hands of the 60 popularly elected Guardians and place about half a dozen highly-paid officials to do the work. It can prolong the Emergency Powers Act, it can do almost anything it likes. But there is **one** thing it cannot do, it cannot pass a law to crush the spirit of Comradeship and Fellowship with all its kindness, love, and sympathy that exists among the workers of this country and the world.

Sympathy is, as is the breath of life, that no legislation can over-rule. This is the Divine in Human Nature which no Government can kill. The work of the 'Women's Committees for the relief of Miners' Wives and Children' in London is an expression of this, also the work of our women and men folk all over the Coalfields.

What a blessing this Fund is to the mothers and babies. Never before in any crisis have we been able to do anything on these lines, and we can thank the Women's Committee for a portion of the funds collected for this special work. The Labour Women's Organisation were called upon to form local Committees with representatives from the Co-operative

Women's Guilds, Midwives Association, and Sisterhoods, and these Committees, under the supervision of the Women's Advisory Councils, are dealing with this work. Whoever the applicants are, and whatever their politics are, if they are wives and children of miners in this lock-out, then they are dealt with.

Here I may point out the real value of 'Organisation'; if we had no women's organisation in the Coalfields, this work could not be done. This Committee have a Children's Department to make arrangements for children to be adopted by comrades in and around London, and other places, during the crisis. Last week we were fortunate to take to London 104 children from South Wales and Monmouthshire Coalfield, and we had such a glorious display of real sympathy which will never be forgotten. The majority of the children were girls, ranging from 7 to 14 years of age. Some of them were from very poor homes with large families, and all of them could do with a change. Some of them had attaché cases and parcels, and on the label carefully written in block letters were 'PASSENGER TO LONDON.' A large number had no luggage, all the clothes they possessed were on them.

What excitement, and oh what joy going to London for the first time. One little girl remarked: 'My father was forty years of age yesterday, he has never been to London, I am only eleven and going there today.' We had reserved coaches on the Railway, and received nothing but kindness from all the Railway men en route. When we reached Paddington the scene was very impressive. Railway men were ready with cups of water to quench their thirst, and one realised the truth of that verse: 'For inasmuch as ye do it unto the least of my little ones, ye have done it unto Me.'

A party of the comrades from Tufton Street met us with Miss Gottsman who is in charge of this Department. The foster mothers and fathers were all waiting with warm hearts to welcome the children, and to make them very happy. The children were lined up, and before dispersing sang 'Hen Wlad fy Nhadau,' as only Welsh children can sing, and which brought tears to the eyes of the onlookers.

Speaking to one of the foster mothers I remarked how very kind the London people were to offer them homes. 'What else can we do,' was the reply, 'I lived in Wales once, and one of my children was born in Gilfach during a strike, and I have never forgotten it.'

Another engine-driver standing by said, 'I have seven kiddies at home, but dash it all, another one will make very little difference. I would like to adopt one.'

A remark was heard that the children from Wales did not look so poorly clad as the little ones who previously came from Somerset.

Little did the onlookers know of the sacrifice that had been made by the mothers of those children to make the children look nice and also to the band of the noble Labour women in the respective areas that had been collecting and making clothes for some of the children who had nothing decent to put on. We were determined that no child should be made an object of poverty for any spectators.

All the children are fixed up quite comfortably and are quite happy, and the letters they have sent home have brought comfort and joy to the parents, and make us all realise that there is a lot of kindness in this world, and it is during a crisis of this kind its resources are felt to the full.

Who knows, maybe these little ones will make life-long friends that will bring them great joy and help in the days to come.

This is, indeed, **something that no Tory Government can quench.**

December 1926

THE COLLIERY WORKER'S MAGAZINE
THE WOMEN'S PAGE

Industrial War and its Aftermath

Industrial war, like every other war in society, has its aftermath. Order out of chaos does not come as soon as the armistice takes place, or when peace terms are ratified. We have to face an aftermath. At the time of penning this article the Mining Crisis looks as if it is coming to an end. **'Not a Settlement'** but a **'Temporary Surrender'** because we are faced with starvation with all its attendant misery.

After seven long months of struggling against the Mineowners and the Government, after seven long months of glorious sacrifice and unprecedented sympathy, we now have to face in Industry longer hours and less wages; in the home, piled up debts, arrears of rent and rates, lack of boots, clothing, and bedclothes; in the Community, Local Authorities and Boards of Guardians piling up debts that we cannot hope to wipe out for years to come.

The work of Local Governing Bodies is held up because they have no money. The education of the children having a set back, and the Tory Minister of Education telling us that it will be impossible for approximately 8,000 children to get Secondary School this year because the children have been fed at School.

Then we have to face the result of the Emergency Powers Act, hundreds of our men and women awaiting trial at the Assizes, and a large number in prison, and all who suffer in this respect are our own people.

The position, when we look around at present, makes one despair, but we must not despair; our pioneers are urging us to carry on, **'there is another day for the workers yet'**, if they will but learn the lesson from this Crisis, and see to it that this will not happen again. There will be no surrender next time to the Mineowners if the Workers will only use their Political Power to get a Labour Government in power.

There is no doubt that the Miners have the sympathy of the other workers in this fight, but with all the sympathy and goodwill in the world, while the political machinery is in the hands of the masters, we are helpless, industrially, and we shall suffer with this mad game.

Our work, therefore, is to carry on propaganda work more vigorous than ever, trying to make every working man and woman politically conscious, and helping them to realise that if they want to save themselves, **'They must mind their own business, politically'**.

We must make the question of the 'Nationalisation of the Mines,' a live subject in any future propaganda work, so as to prepare the minds of the people for the great change that must inevitably take place in the mining industry before Peace, Contentment and Prosperity can be achieved.

The Work of Women

The work of the National Women's Committee, with its Secretary, Dr Marion Phillips, will never be forgotten, neither will the work of the noble bands of women in all the mining areas be forgotten, as well as the noble work of 'The Society of Friends,' who put their religion into practice wherever there is need.

We have been the 'Red Cross Nurses,' doing the 'Red Cross Work' in this war. Alleviating distress here, bringing succour there, but all the time paying the greatest attention to the weakest members of the fight – **the sick mothers and babies**.

We shall have to continue with our 'Red Cross Work,' and dedicate ourselves to work for the future, for the bringing in of a state of society where a war of this kind will never be needed, because we have been wise enough to use our Political Power to capture the machinery of Government from our oppressors.

THE COLLIERY WORKER'S MAGAZINE
THE WOMEN'S PAGE

Ring out the Old – Ring in the New

A Happy New Year to All

By the time this article will be in the hands of our readers, the bells will have rung out the Old Year, 1926, and rung in the New, 1927.

Notwithstanding all our difficulties, we must look forward with renewed Hope and Courage, and trust that some new avenue will open so that Peace and Security can be established.

The Industrial War that we have just passed through has maimed thousands of our young mothers and babies, and has undermined the health of the children, and our womenfolk and our men folk.

An Industrial War of this kind is more cruel than a Military War, because its victims are slowly starved and tortured physically and mentally.

Ring out the old – Ring in the new

To change all this we must this New Year **ring out of our minds** old ideas, old traditions, old customs, old prejudices, jealousies, suspicion, **and ring in the new** ideals, the newer conception of what life should be, and **must be**; a newer conception of our relationship with each other, and our duties, putting in the forefront all the time and every time the claim of 'The Child.'

If we could only approach all our Economic, Social, National and International problems from this point of view, **making the welfare of the Child the basis of human relationship in Human Society**, we would soon solve these problems.

One great writer says: 'That the 18th Century found the Man, the 19th Century found the Woman, but the 20th Century would find the child. It was going to be the Children's Era.'

When we look around we find traces of this new spirit in every phase of life. Health matters, Housing, Education, Recreation, Habits, Customs, Environment, are all factors that are now dealt with from this standpoint these last few years.

The new science of Psychology has revolutionised old ideas that we had on these problems, and we can see the foundation of this new era laid through the plastic mind of the Child.

We have experienced a little of this wonderful spirit pervading the work done in this crisis. It has been very wonderful, caring for the Child through co-operative effort; the months of hard work, cutting up old garments and making them into new for the children, so as to clothe them, and looking after the mothers and babies and the invalid children, the adoption of our children with comrades in and around London, have opened up a tremendous avenue of fellowship and comradeship, and a relationship that will never be forgotten. Not only caring for them with food and raiment, but their education and health; and many of them have had the best medical attention during their stay; whereas they went away ailing, they have returned full of vigour and renewed health.

The work done by our men at Bootrepairing Centres is part of all this wonderful work — a labour of love. Thousands of children's boots have been repaired to make it possible for the children to be shod.

What is underlying this wonderful spirit? It is the spirit of the New Era – the care of the Child, not only individually but collectively.

This spirit must be developed and maintained in normal times. It will help us to bring nearer the dreams of our Pioneers, so let us Ring Out the Old, and Ring In the New in the truest sense this New Year.

> Ring out old shapes of foul disease,
> Ring out the narrowing lust of gold;
> Ring out the thousand wars of old,
> Ring in the thousand years of peace.
>
> Ring in the valiant man and free,
> The larger heart, the kindlier hand;
> Ring out the darkness of the land,
> Ring in the Christ that is to be.

May 1927

THE COLLIERY WORKER'S MAGAZINE
THE WOMEN'S PAGE

'Votes for Women'

'Votes for Women' has again become within the realm of practical politics this last few weeks.

The Tory Prime Minister last week announced in the House that he intended bringing in a Government Bill, before the end of the year, to give Votes for Women at 21 years of age, and that if this Government will continue in office until the end of the term, that the women will be able to exercise their Vote at the next General Election.

This is good news to the women, **but** we must 'wait and see' whether this promise will be carried out, for **Tory promises are like pie-crusts – made to be broken**.

There has been much writing in the Press on this matter, and some of the Old Fogies in the Political World are greatly perturbed and have raised the scare of 'Votes for Flappers,' as if all the women between the ages of 21 years and 30 years of age are the most irresponsible people in the world.

They forget that at least 80 per cent of these women are the daughters and wives of workers, some of them doing their share in Industry and other occupations, and the majority of them young mothers, with little ones to care for. Surely these women are capable of exercising their vote and to have a voice in the laws that govern them in the Home and in Industry.

Some men fear **'Petticoat Government'**, as if the women could make a worse mess of Politics than has been done in the past. There will be two million more women voters in this country than men when this Bill becomes law – hence this fear.

Press Arguments

All sorts of arguments are raised in the Press and by people who do not believe in Political Equality. One argument deals with the added expense of Elections, whereas now it costs approximately £800 for each Parliament candidature, this Bill will meanb an added £100 to £160 to each Parliamentary Division. What if it does; it is better for us to spend on the Vote Weapon than on the War Weapons. It is saner, cheaper, more humane and more consistent with 20th Century civilisation.

The other argument is that the Bill is uncalled for, that the young women are not asking for votes. These people forget that Adult Suffrage has been agitated for since the first Reform Bill, 1832, and nearly a century ago the pioneers of the Labour Party, and the Labour Party, in season and out of season, in the House and on public platforms, have consistently carried on this agitation, because we believe in Political Equality.

This Bill will be an important factor, not only for the younger women between the ages of 21 years and 30 years, but to all us older women, who have been privileged to use the Vote. **It will raise our status as Voters**, and remove that insult to our womanhood that we got Votes because we are **married to men**, not because we were intelligent human beings and citizens. The qualification for the unmarried spinster of 30 years is that of owning **two rooms and furniture**.

There are two million women over 30 years who had no votes because of this ridiculous qualification – **two rooms and furniture** – whatever profession or work they did in the community.

This promised Bill will remove this anomaly as well, and place these two million women on the Register, as well as three million women between the ages of 21 years to 30 years, of which 60 per cent of the latter will be over 25 years of age.

The majority of these new women voters have been workers in Industry, Business or Domestic Service, at least seven years before they reach the age of 21 years, and a large number have had to be little mothers in the home long before the age of 14 years.

So the cry, **'Votes for Flappers'**, is an insult to these women.

Let us therefore do all we can to help our younger women, as well as ourselves, for Political Equality. We can do this by creating public opinion, so that when the Bill is before the House, the House will realise that it must carry it through.

October 1935

THE RHONDDA CLARION
NO. 2

A Clarion Call — To the Rhondda Women

The Rhondda Clarion is launching out on its second edition. We hope it will fill that long-felt need in the Rhondda Valley, for accurate facts, and reports of the activities of the Urban Council and County Council, that affects our lives so closely, as well as the Labour Party's work in Parliament and in the country generally.

May I, at the outset, make an appeal to all our Women's Sections and Ward Councils to make 'The Clarion' a huge success, by ensuring a wide circulation, and also by making it the source of information; and thus help to clear the atmosphere that has been so polluted in the Rhondda, by misstatements, half-truths, suspicion, and misrepresentation, created by the propaganda of the Communist Party this last number of years.

We must learn to know the difference between a big noise and steady work, between walking out and creating scenes in the Council Chambers and facing facts and difficulties of administration and obtaining the maximum out of every Act of Parliament for the common good.

It is the PLODDERS that do the work of the WORLD, not the SHOUTERS.

J. Bruce Glasier, one of our Socialist pioneers, emphasised a very sound philosophy when he said: 'You cannot boil a kettle by rattling the lid. But you boil the kettle and the lid will rattle alright'.

This is very apt to the work of the Rhondda Council at present. We have a few who are there to do nothing but 'rattle lids' (by instruction) but the work of the Council is done day in and day out in a quiet but constructive way. These are difficult times and many problems demand our serious attention both locally and nationally. Let "The Clarion" be our guide in the future.

War Clouds

Black war clouds are hovering over us the last few weeks because there is a Big Boisterous and Ambitious Brother among the family of nations that wants to dominate and destroy a smaller and weaker Brother, and the rest of the family have been called in to decide what action they will take to protect the weaker brother.

Public opinion in this country has compelled a Tory Government at last to stand by the Covenant of the League of Nations. This crisis is the challenge of a Dictator to the Collective Peace System built up since the last war – to end war.

There are other dark clouds at home, that need our serious attention. These clouds threaten us with an industrial war. But this will be a war that calls us all to take part in this fight because it is not a war to kill, burn and destroy, but a war against Poverty. A just demand, so that miners get a square deal.

We need hundred per cent Trade Unionism, hundred per cent Loyalty, and we shall win. The women can play a great part in this fight, so let us be up and doing, helping the Miners' Federation locally and nationally in the campaign.

War and Poverty are the Twin Evils of the present system. Both are man-made and both can be eradicated when the workers WILL IT, and use their power to bring about the desired change.

LABOUR WOMAN

Bread and Peace

'Swords shall be turned in to ploughshares
and spears into pruning-hooks'

How many times has this prophecy been quoted from pulpit and from platform in every country where the Christian gospel is preached!

How many to-day believe it possible? In these days of armament building, we almost despair of its realisation.

Poverty and War

Our own Government with its stupid international policy which has led to the squandering of the nation's wealth on armaments , and the mortgaging of the nation's future, will lead us to destruction unless the people wake up and cry halt.

Wars here and dictators there – that is the order of the day. Where there are wars and dictators we have cruelty, tyranny, suppression and fear.

Yet we know that underlying all these evils is the problem of poverty.

Starvation in Japan – Underfeeding in Britain

Kagwa knows this in Japan and he preaches and pleads for international co-operation as one way out. Japan has the densest population in the world. Seventy million people try to live in a country of 10,000 square miles, only 15 per cent of which is arable land. In Japan there are hundreds of family pact suicides every year, whole families agreeing to end their lives because they see no way to avoid starvation.

But the problem of preventing starvation is not confined to Japan. It is world wide.

We see it in this country in the too meagre pensions to the old folk, widows and orphans, inadequate unemployment insurance and U.A.B. allowances, as well as in the low wages paid to many sections of the workers, which make it impossible for the people to get the food necessary to maintain health.

The Unsolved Problem

We have solved the problems of production and transport – every problem indeed but the problem of satisfying human needs. We welcome the statements of experts like Sir John Orr and Julian Huxley and others who are devoting themselves to the problem of nutrition.

In the report of the Director of the International Labour Office for 1936, we read that 'War is not only or mainly caused by lust of territory or booty or prestige, but it is also caused by low standards of living, by the feeling of economic insecurity, by the desire for moral and social emancipation. The founders of the International Labour Office were right when they discerned a lasting connection between peace and social justice'.

Adequate Diet

Douglas Jay, City Editor of the 'Daily Herald', in a recent article on a food plan to end malnutrition showed that if all the people in this country could get an adequate diet, as suggested, for example, by Sir John Orr, we would need to spend £105 millions more on food per year, if prices remained at the present level. We need to spend that amount more on protective foods - £30 millions on fruit, £10 millions on vegetables, £14 millions on milk, £7½ millions on eggs, £8 millions on butter, £35 millions on meat.

Goering said to the German people 'You cannot have guns and butter.'

This Government is indirectly telling us that we cannot have an increased standard of living and armaments.

A Frontal Attack on Poverty

There is a way out. Instead of nations fighting each other and preparing to destroy each other, they could devote their energies and resources to fighting poverty in each country. The League of Nations could play a great part in this work. The reports published by the League Nutrition Committee are a challenge to the world to find social and economic salvation in healthy well-fed peoples.

Labour's policy in agriculture stands for the same ideal. Everyone should read 'Your Britain' No. 3 on Food and Farming.

If all Governments, aided by their experts, realised the real nature of the problem and were determined to solve it, we could in our time realise the prophecy with which I began this article. For we could turn the material resources at present being devoted to war preparations to use in feeding the peoples of the world and in raising standards of living.

Swords into Ploughshares

Steel, iron and other minerals were never meant to destroy mankind. Cotton and wool are not meant to feed guns, but to clothe human beings. Arable land is meant to produce food. We are told that even the gases that are prepared for war could be used as fertilisers to bring greater production from the land.

The aeroplanes that are made to carry bombs could become messengers for trade and goodwill among the nations of the world.

The more we give thought to the problems of nutrition and poverty, the more significant becomes the old proverb about turning swords into ploughshares.

Labour women have taken up this question of nutrition and the standard of living with great determination. To all those who are really interested in nutrition and who truly desire peace, I would say that Labour's policy is the only way out of poverty at home and war abroad. They must join with us in turning this race in armaments into a race for security against poverty.

LABOUR WOMAN

Wales and her Poverty

For the last few months the Report of the Inquiry into Anti-Tuberculosis Services in Wales and Monmouth has had a great deal of publicity from Press and platforms.

We know that there are several factors that account for this disease, but we also know, as Socialists, that poverty is one of the chief causes.

Poverty and Tuberculosis

It is surprising how Anti-Socialists and 'non-political' speakers give great emphasis to the factors which coincide with their views and outlook. The women are blamed by some, and are told they do not know how to cook, but the average woman's reply is: **'Give us something to cook, and we will show you that we can do it'**.

Low Wages, Unemployment Insurance Benefit and Means Test allowances allow very little for food, when rent has been paid. So we maintain that poverty is the main factor. Nutrition and environment depend on wages.

Tuberculosis attacks the young particularly as facts and figures in the Report make plain. Our adolescents are not having the quantity and quality of food that nature needs for body building. Right food is the essential basis for the health of our future citizens. Young mothers die from TB because of the strain of motherhood under poverty.

Our Labour women in Wales welcome this Report and will carry on a campaign during the coming months. We must see to it that this document does not meet the same fate as many previous reports by being pigeon-holed in Whitehall and Council Offices.

Social Services

In discussing the causes of the excessive Tuberculosis rate, Labour women are raising wider social issues, and emphasise the necessity of constructively planned social services: Nutrition, Maternity and Child Welfare Clinics, Dental Clinics, Nursery Schools, School Meals, School Equipment and amenities, School Medical Services, Housing, Sanitation, Clean Water, Clean Milk, etc.

These are vital factors in any scheme for the prevention of Tuberculosis. Our first duty is to see what can be done immediately to check its ravages, and we are urging Local Authorities generally, and backward Local Authorities especially, to speed up their Social Services. In connection, with free milk and meals for school children we say that underfeeding should be the test, not diagnosed malnutrition. A child may be insufficiently fed because of its parents' poverty a long time before a doctor can detect malnutrition.

Water Supply

We are also urging Government Grants to help the Local Authorities with Housing and Sanitation. Good sanitation depends on a good water supply which is lacking in many of the agricultural counties. For example, Anglesey is the third county on the black list. The people there depend for their water supply on wells; yet across the Menai Straits we have the Snowdonian Mountains with lakes of pure soft water which supply many cities in England. It will cost the Anglesey County £500,000 to get a supply from this source across the

Straits and they are too poor to get the job done. A penny rate for the whole County only produces £633! To find even half of the £500,000 would mean a rate of £1 12s 10d per £!

Water is nature's gift to mankind – it falls like manna from the heavens – no cost for production, only for storage and distribution. A pure water supply should be a national responsibility. Drought, floods and shortage are a real menace to health and life because we have not yet had the wisdom to harness and store the rainfall.

Clean Milk

Clean milk is another factor that falls for special attention. Tubercular cattle should be destroyed and the farmer compensated. Rigid supervision and inspection of cattle are urgently needed.

We need more Sanatoria to isolate cases to prevent the spreading of the disease. Then, last but not least, is the aftercare of T.B. patients. Each authority should be compelled to appoint qualified nurses to deal with this work and adequate nourishment should be provided for the patients and their dependants.

We have much propaganda work to do on this report and we shall have to be audacious and persistent in our propaganda to get something done. There is an old Welsh saying, **'Dyfal donc y dyr y garreg'**, which means **'It is steady knocking that breaks the stone'**. This is our motto in the present campaign.

February 1948

LABOUR WOMAN

Wales — Then and Now: 1919-1947

ON DECEMBER 15TH, 1947, I retired from the post of Organiser for Wales, after 28 years and nine months' service. During this period we have experienced many *ups* and *downs* and *downs* and *ups* in the development of our Movement.

A brief review will be helpful to remind us how far we have travelled thus and teach us the way we should go, in the next step in this march of progress.

During the 1914-18 World War, the women were called upon to play their part. This gave them an opportunity to serve on various commitees as well as in wartime industries.

But women generally were very shy of politics; they were nervous about being called a Suffragette or a Socialist. The partial Franchise to women of 30 years did open the door to women to take part in public life, and break down the barriers that prevented women being Members of Parliament, Councillors and Magistrates.

When the Labour Party widened its basis of membership, so that women could join as Individual Members, and they appointed Dr. Marion Phillips as Chief Women's Officer, and a few women organisers, the women's side of our organisation began to grow.

We went out as missionaries (with very little equipment, but with a great missionary zeal), preaching this new Gospel of Social Justice and a new way of life. The responsibility of Citizenship and the Power through the Ballot Box was the burden of our song.

It was the mining valleys of South Wales that responded first, the Miners' Federation had three political agents in South Wales, and that gave me considerable help to organise the miners wives'. The interest soon spread to the towns and villages, and thus, week by week, we developed Women's Sections in some Division or other (before Ward Parties were formed).

Local Elections became of great interest to the women, and the Parliamentary Election meetings were enthusiastic and lively, the workers wives had at last been aroused and given a chance to express themselves. Some of the by-elections in this area will always stand out vividly in my mind. Mass canvassing with a bell, street and cottage meetings, and the colour display on election day was very exciting; the children dressed up and, with their improvised bands, played a great part in arousing enthusiasm. Women canvassers lent their coats and shoes for some of the poorest women to go and vote, and minded their babies. It was this spirit and sacrifice that made South Wales a stronghold for Labour.

The development of Advisory Councils was a grand idea to co-ordinate the educational work, and bring people together from mining valleys, towns and villages, and giving them a broader outlook and a wider vision of the needs of women and the work of the Party, and its organisation. It also helped to train our women to play an active part in election work through our one-day, weekend and summer schools, and also equipped them with knowledge to become Councillors. We are very proud of the number of Women Councillors and Magistrates we have in Wales.

We developed a Pageant on many occasions for Women's Month, which was a very effective way of demonstrating our views on many problems.

Travelling was very difficult in the early days, and money scarce. Nevertheless, the enthusiasm, sincerity and faith of our women comrades helped us to overcome all our difficulties.

This is a brief sketch of the work done. We have now reached a new phase in our work. So many of the things we worked for, hoped for and prayed for are achieved, or about to be achieved as a result of the work of the Labour Government. But our work has not finished; indeed, our responsibility increases daily if Social Democracy is going to be a success in this country.

First of all I would suggest that each member will try and get well-informed on the Government's achievements, and all the Acts that come into force in 1948. Next, we must make every member feel proud that they belong to the Labour Party, and be loyal to our leaders and our Government, and make every member, and supporter feel that if they cast a vote for Labour in the 1945 election, or did any work to help in this election, be it great or small, that they share the credit with the Government in their achievement.

In this spirit we can go out to make converts, as well as making ourselves better members of the Party, and build up a better organisation in each Division.

We must train our future representatives, whether for Parliament or Councils. We must also train our future officers.

There is a cultural side of our Movement that we must develop if we accept this new way of life. There is also a very human side that we must not neglect; we are not only a Party machine, but a great human movement.

In conclusion, may I offer in great humility my sincerest thanks to all the officers and Section members, Advisory Councils, Central Committees and Federations, and officers of the Party generally in Wales, for long years of loyal comradeship and fellowship, and helpful co-operation in my work. I feel sure you will give to my successor the same loyalty and co-operation you have given me all these years.

While I say adieu officially, I hope I shall be spared for many years to help with the educational work of the Party.

Wishing you all a very happy and prosperous year.

> *'The journey is done, and the summit is attained*
> *And the banners fall.*
> *Though the battle's to fight, ere the guerdon be gained —*
> *The reward of it all.*
> *I was ever a fighter so. One fight more,*
> *The best and the last.'*
>
> Browning

Historical Autobiographies from Honno

A popular series covering Welsh women's experiences from the economic depression of the 1920s through to the post war decades of the 1950s and 60s.

Highly readable and a key resource for the study of Welsh Women's History.

Struggle or Starve

Women's Lives in the South Wales Valleys between the Two World Wars ed. Carol White and Sian Rhiannon Williams

"a book to treasure" The Big Issue Cymru

ISBN 1 870206 258; £9.95

Parachutes and Petticoats

Welsh Women writing on the Second World War ed. Leigh Verrill-Rhys and Deirdre Beddoe

"A marvellous compilation of reminiscences by Welsh women" Time Out

ISBN 1 870206 126; £9.99

Iancs, Conshis a Spam

Atgofion Menywod o'r Ail Ryfel Byd gol./ed. Leigh Verrill-Rhys

ISBN 1 87206 428; £ 9.99

Changing Times

Welsh Women writing on the 1950s and 60s ed. Deirdre Beddoe

"All these stories are fascinating and astonishingly diverse; sometimes hair-raising, sometimes humorous, each one touchingly atmospheric." Planet

ISBN 1 870206 533   £ 9.99

Other titles in theHonno Classics series

Iron and Gold
By Hilda Vaughan
Introduction by Jane Aaron
ISBN 1 870206 50 9
£8.99

The Wooden Doctor
By Margiad Evans
Introduction by Dr Sue
Asbee
ISBN 1 870206 68 1
£6.99

The Small Mine
By Menna Gallie
Introduction by Professor
Angela John
ISBN 1 870206 38 X
£6.99

Strike for a Kingdom
By Menna Gallie
Introduction by Professor
Angela John
ISBN 1 870206 58 4
£6.99

Eunice Fleet
By Lily Tobias
Introduction by Dr Jasmine
Donahaye
ISBN 1 870206 65 7
£8.99

A View Across the Valley:
Short stories by women
from Wales c1859-1950
Ed Professor Jane Aaron
ISBN 1 870206 35 5
£7.95

Queen of the Rushes:A
Tale of the Welsh Revival
By Allen Raine
ISBN 1 870206 29 0
£7.95

The Rebecca Rioter
By Amy Dillwyn
Introduction by Dr Katie
Gramich
ISBN 1 870206 43 6
£8.99

Welsh Women's Poetry
1460 - 2001: An Anthology
Eds Dr Katie Gramich and
Catherine Brennan
ISBN 1 870206 54 1
£12.99